Simple One-Pot Stews

Also by Maria Robbins

The Dumpling Cookbook

American Corn

Blue-Ribbon Cookies

Blue-Ribbon Pies

Blue-Ribbon Pickles and Preserves

A Cook's Alphabet of Quotations

The Christmas Companion (with Jim Charlton)

A Gardener's Bouquet of Quotations

Cookies for Christmas

Chili!

Baking for Christmas

Chocolate for Christmas

Biscotti and Other Low-Fat Cookies

The One-Dish Vegetarian

 ST. MARTIN'S GRIFFIN   NEW YORK

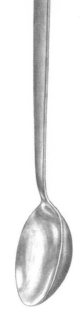

Simple One-Pot Stews

Delicious, Satisfying Stews
from Around the World, for the
Stove Top or Slow Cooker

Maria Robbins

Design by Susan Walsh
Illustrations by Kathryn Parise

www.stmartins.com

ISBN 0-312-24312-X

First Edition: January 2004

10   9   8   7   6   5   4   3   2   1

Contents

	Introduction	ix
one	Vegetable Stews	1
two	Fish and Seafood Stews	17
three	Chicken Stews	41
four	Veal Stews	57
five	Beef Stews	75
six	Lamb Stews	95
seven	Pork Stews	117
	Index	135

Introduction

Stews have surely been around for as long as humans have had pots to cook in. Put some meat, a vegetable if you've got one, and some (but not too much) water into a pot and cook until the meat is very tender—and you've got a stew not so different from those of prehistoric times! Today's stews may require a little more preparation and a few more ingredients, but basically they are as easy to prepare as in the dim past, but with results that are much more flavorful and varied.

Because stew recipes are so easy to make, so hearty and satisfying, so good the next day, and so easy to freeze, I've been collecting them for years—organizing and reorganizing my gustatory database by whim and happenstance as much as by flavors or ingredients. What follows is a big, bubbling potful of my current as well as long-standing favorites.

Some are classics—not exactly sacrosanct, but certainly time-honored to the extent that their basic lineaments should not be much altered. Others are not so much classics as basics—simple, sturdy, and adaptable—virtually begging for improvisation.

Stewing is by nature a slow way of cooking, which is not to say that it is labor intensive—indeed, most of the wonderful, slow-simmering time involved will not require any effort on your part at all. Still, most of the stews in this book, except for the fish, seafood,

chicken, and vegetable stews, will take several hours to cook. Except for the fish, seafood, and vegetable stews, all can be made a day or two ahead and refrigerated until you are ready to serve them, and many actually improve in flavor when made ahead and given time to rest.

Vegetable stews are best served on the same day you make them, but most can be served either hot or at room temperature. Don't refrigerate a vegetable stew before serving or it will lose some of its flavor.

A few technical notes:

- An electric slow cooker can be used to prepare the chicken, veal, beef, lamb, and pork stews in this book. You should brown the meat as described in the recipe, sauté the vegetables, combine with the liquid and seasoning, and transfer to the cooker. Follow the cooker directions, if you have them, for the timing. Most cookers have a high and low setting. If you choose high, cook the stew for five to six hours; if low, cook for eight to ten hours. Stir the stew a couple of times during the cooking process, but don't remove the lid for long or you will lose too much heat.

- Most stews are best prepared in a large, heavy pot. My preference has always been an enameled cast-iron Dutch oven, preferably made by Le Creuset.

- Browning the meat before stewing it adds substantial flavor to the meat and the sauce. It is an important first step, but you don't have to be too fussy about it. If you brown the meat well on one or two sides, that's good enough. The browned flavor will come through.

- I will often double a stew recipe and freeze half for a future meal. Having a prepared meal in the freezer is like having money in the bank.

- When a stew calls for wine, try to use the same wine that you will serve with the stew. The flavor of the wine will be the dominant flavor of the stew. If you use a bad wine, you will have a bad stew.

Simple One-Pot Stews

Vegetable Stews

Spring Vegetable Stew

This lovely springtime stew is based on a recipe in Deborah Madison's wonderful book Vegetarian Cooking for Everyone. *One thing to keep in mind when making this recipe is that the blanching times are approximate, and you should blanch the vegetables to the doneness that you like. Most people like their vegetables to be slightly crispy, just underdone. But some like their vegetables to be completely cooked through. Just don't overcook them too much. Serve the stew with a loaf of crispy crusted French bread and some good butter.*

Serves 6

18 baby carrots
9 radishes, including $1/2$ inch of stems, cut in half through the stems
24 3-inch asparagus tips
9 scallions, including green stems, cut into 3-inch lengths
3 broccoli stems, thickly peeled and sliced on the diagonal
4 small turnips, peeled and cut into sixths
1 cup fresh or frozen peas, thawed
4 tablespoons unsalted butter
1 tablespoon fresh thyme leaves
1 tablespoon fresh lemon juice
Salt and freshly ground black pepper
1 tablespoon chopped chives
1 tablespoon finely chopped parsley
1 tablespoon chopped tarragon
10 sorrel leaves, thinly sliced (optional)

1. In a large pot bring 3 quarts of water to a boil together with 1 tablespoon of salt. Add the carrots, blanch them for 3 to 4 minutes, and remove them with a slotted spoon to a bowl. Blanch the remaining vegetables, one type at a time: radishes, 2 to 3 minutes; asparagus tips 2 to 3 minutes; scallions, 1 minute; broccoli stems, 2 to 3 minutes; turnips, 3 to 4 minutes; and peas, 1 minute. Reserve 1½ cups of the cooking water and discard the rest.

2. In a large deep-sided skillet, melt the butter together with the thyme leaves and the reserved cooking liquid over medium-high heat.

3. Add the vegetables and simmer, uncovered, over medium heat until the vegetables are completely warmed through, 3 to 5 minutes. Add the lemon juice and season to taste with salt and pepper. Add the sorrel (if using) and the remaining herbs, and cook for 1 minute more. Serve hot or at room temperature. Do not refrigerate.

Summer Vegetable Stew

Here I bring together a simple succotash with some other summer vegetables to make a delicious stew. It is perfect for late summer, when fresh corn, peppers, and ripe tomatoes are readily available.

Serves 4 to 6

> 1 quart water
> 2 cups fresh shelled cranberry beans, or 1 10-ounce package frozen baby
>   lima beans, thawed
> 4 tablespoons unsalted butter
> 2 medium red onions, finely chopped
> 1 red bell pepper, cored, seeded, and diced
> 1 zucchini, quartered lengthwise and diced
> 3 cups fresh corn kernels from 4 ears of shucked corn
> 1 large tomato, peeled, seeded, and diced
> 1/4 cup heavy cream or crème fraîche
> Salt and freshly ground black pepper

1. Bring the water to a boil in a medium pot and add the fresh or frozen beans. Cook for 5 to 10 minutes until the beans are tender and drain.

2. Melt the butter over medium-high heat in a large deep-sided skillet. Add the onions and red pepper and sauté for 5 minutes, until softened. Add the zucchini, corn, tomato, and cream or crème fraîche. Cook, stirring frequently, for about 10 minutes, until all vegetables are cooked. Season with salt and pepper to taste. Serve hot or at room temperature. Do not refrigerate.

Autumn Vegetable Stew

The most time-consuming element of this recipe is the need to cut the vegetables into ¼-inch pieces. But it's worth the effort. Serve with crusty bread and butter.

Serves 6

> **2 large carrots, peeled**
> **2 medium turnips, peeled**
> **2 medium parsnips, peeled**
> **2 large leeks, dark green ends and outer skins removed, and washed**
> **8 scallions, outer skins removed, and washed**
> **1 large butternut squash, outer peel and seeds removed, cut into large chunks**
> **1 small celery root, outer skin cut away, placed in water to cover with lemon juice**
> **2 medium kohlrabies, about ½ pound, outer skins peeled away (optional)**
> **1½ pounds Yukon Gold potatoes, peeled and placed in water to cover**
> **6 tablespoons unsalted butter**
> **Salt and freshly ground black pepper**
> **¼ cup finely chopped inner light green celery leaves**
> **1 quart chicken broth or vegetable stock**
> **2 garlic cloves, finely chopped**
> **½ cup fresh marjoram leaves**
> **⅓ cup chopped Italian parsley**

1. Cut all the vegetables into ¼-inch pieces.
2. In a large deep-sided skillet or sauté pan, melt the butter over medium-high heat until it foams. Add the carrots, turnips,

parsnips, leeks, scallions, squash, celery root, and kohlrabies, stir, and cook, covered, until vegetables are a little soft, about 15 minutes. Season to taste with salt and pepper. Stir in the chopped celery leaves, add the chicken broth, and simmer uncovered, for 5 minutes.

3. Add the potatoes and the garlic and simmer 15 minutes longer, until the potatoes are cooked through. Add the marjoram and parsley. Taste for seasoning and adjust. Serve hot or at room temperature. Do not refrigerate.

Winter Vegetable Stew

This hearty, satisfying stew is full of deep, sweet flavors balanced by the slight bitterness of the greens and the tangy flavor of the lime juice.

Serves 6

1 small butternut squash, peeled, seeded, and cut into 1-inch cubes
8 medium shallots, peeled
1 tablespoon olive oil
Salt and freshly ground black pepper
6 medium parsnips, peeled and cut into 2-inch pieces
4 small turnips, peeled and quartered
4 medium carrots, cut into 2-inch pieces
½ pound small Yukon Gold or red-skinned potatoes, peeled and quartered
2 large leeks, dark green ends removed, cut in half lengthwise and sliced across into 2-inch pieces
1 large bunch Swiss chard, washed, leaves cut away from stems, stems cut across into 1-inch slices, and leaves cut across into ¼-inch-wide strips
3 cups chicken broth
2 tablespoons unsalted butter
1 teaspoon fresh thyme leaves
2 tablespoons freshly squeezed lime juice

1. Preheat the oven to 400° F.
2. Place the butternut squash and shallots into a shallow roasting pan and toss with the olive oil. Season with salt and pepper and roast for about 30 minutes, until both vegetables are tender.

3. In a large sauté pan or Dutch oven combine the parsnips, turnips, carrots, potatoes, leeks, Swiss chard stems, chicken broth, butter, and thyme. Bring to a boil over medium-high heat, reduce heat to low, cover, and simmer for 10 minutes.

4. Stir in the chard leaves, add a little water if necessary, cover, and continue to simmer until all vegetables are tender, about 10 to 12 minutes.

5. Add the roasted squash and shallots to the stew, season to taste with salt and pepper, sprinkle with lime juice, and serve.

Lentil, Potato, and Spinach Stew

The lentils, potatoes, and spinach make a rich and very tasty combination. The carrots add a little sweetness and the mint and lemon juice add a lightness to the stew. You can make it a day before serving without any loss of flavor or freshness.

Serves 4

3 tablespoons olive oil
6 garlic cloves, finely minced or pushed through a garlic press
6 cups chicken broth
2 cups lentils, picked over and rinsed
1 pound Yukon Gold or red-skinned potatoes, cut into $1/2$-inch pieces
2 medium carrots, cut into $1/2$-inch pieces
12 ounces fresh spinach leaves, washed, dried, and torn into pieces
2 tablespoons freshly squeezed lemon juice
$1/2$ teaspoon grated lemon peel
$1/4$ teaspoon cayenne
1 tablespoon chopped fresh mint
Salt and freshly ground black pepper

1. Put the oil in a large Dutch oven and place over medium heat. Add the garlic and sauté, stirring for 1 minute. Add the chicken broth and lentils and bring to a boil. Reduce heat to low, cover, and simmer for 10 minutes.

2. Add potatoes and carrots, raise the heat to medium, and simmer, uncovered, until lentils and vegetables are tender, 15 to 20 minutes.
3. Stir in the spinach leaves, lemon juice, lemon peel, and cayenne. Cover and simmer over medium-low heat for 2 to 3 minutes, until the spinach has wilted. Stir in the mint and season with salt and pepper to taste.

Green Bean, Chickpea, Potato, and Zucchini Stew

This recipe is based on a Greek vegetable stew. It can be served hot or at room temperature. Feta cheese and crusty bread are great accompaniments.

Serves 6

1/4 cup olive oil
1 large yellow onion, finely chopped
1 pound fresh green beans, trimmed and cut in half crosswise
1/2 pound Yukon Gold or red-skinned potatoes, peeled and cut into 1-inch cubes
2 medium zucchini, cut into 1-inch slices
1 28-ounce can Italian-style tomatoes, drained and chopped
3/4 cup chopped parsley
1/4 teaspoon cayenne
2 cups chicken broth
2 cups canned, drained, and rinsed chickpeas
Salt and freshly ground black pepper

1. Place the oil in a large deep-sided skillet or sauté pan over medium-high heat. Add the onion and sauté until softened, about 5 minutes. Add the green beans and sauté another 3 minutes, until the onion is translucent.
2. Add the potatoes, zucchini, tomatoes, parsley, cayenne, and chicken broth. Bring to a boil, reduce heat to medium-low, cover,

and simmer for 20 minutes, stirring frequently. Stir in the chickpeas, cover, and simmer another 10 minutes, until the potatoes are tender.

3. Season to taste with salt and pepper. Remove from heat and serve.

Black Bean Chili

I based this recipe on one of the favorites from my book Chili!*, which was published many years ago and is out of print. The addition of chocolate may sound strange, but it gives this vegetarian chili a rich depth of flavor that will make even the most ardent carnivore forget about meat. The bulgur provides a background texture similar to that of ground beef. It is an excellent dish to serve at a party where you'll be hosting both vegetarian and nonvegetarian friends.*

Serves 8 to 10

$1/4$ cup olive oil

2 large onions, coarsely chopped

6 garlic cloves, finely minced or pushed through a garlic press

2 large red bell peppers, cored, seeded, and coarsely chopped

1 large yellow bell pepper, cored, seeded, and coarsely chopped

1 fresh jalapeño chili, cored, seeded, and finely chopped

2 tablespoons ancho chili powder

1 tablespoon ground cumin

4 cups vegetable broth or water

$1/2$ cup bulgur

1 ounce (1 square) unsweetened chocolate, grated

1 28-ounce can tomatoes, drained and coarsely chopped

4 15-ounce cans (about 8 cups) black beans, rinsed and drained

2 cups fresh or frozen corn kernels, thawed

Salt and freshly ground black pepper

For Red Onion Salsa:
4 red onions, finely chopped
4 tablespoons coarse salt
1 cup finely chopped cilantro
2 jalapeño chilies, cored, seeded, and finely chopped
2 to 3 tablespoons freshly squeezed lime juice

1. Prepare the chili: Heat the oil in a large Dutch oven over medium heat. Add the onions and garlic and cook, stirring, for 5 minutes, until the onions have wilted. Add the bell peppers, jalapeño, chili powder, and cumin and cook, stirring, for 3 to 5 minutes longer, until the peppers have softened.

2. Add the vegetable broth or water, bulgur, grated chocolate, tomatoes, and beans. Bring to a boil, lower the heat, and simmer gently for 25 minutes. Add the corn kernels, stir, and simmer for 5 minutes longer. Season to taste with salt and pepper. Remove from the heat and let rest.

3. Prepare the Red Onion Salsa: Place the onions in a large bowl and toss together with the salt. Add enough ice water to just cover the onions. Let stand for 30 minutes.

4. Drain the onions and place in a dry mixing bowl. Add the cilantro, jalapeño chilies, and lime juice. Mix well and serve as a topping for the chili.

two

Fish and Seafood Stews

Catalan Seafood Stew

A friend introduced me to this stew twenty years ago, and it has been in my dinner party repertoire ever since. The Pernod and pine nuts in this recipe add an intense aroma and flavor, and you don't need more than some rice to sop up the juices and a green salad to accompany it.

Serves 4

$^1/_4$ cup olive oil
4 garlic cloves, finely chopped
$1^1/_2$ tablespoons all-purpose flour
1 cup clam juice or fish stock
$^1/_2$ cup Pernod
1 cup chopped fresh or canned tomatoes
$^1/_2$ cup chopped fresh parsley
1 bay leaf
$^1/_4$ teaspoon red pepper flakes (or more to taste)
$^1/_2$ cup pine nuts, toasted in a skillet and pulverized in a food processor
$1^1/_2$ pounds monk, tile, or blackfish (or a combination), cut into bite-size pieces
1 pound shrimp or scallops
Salt and freshly ground black pepper

1. Place a Dutch oven or other stew-type pot over medium heat and add the olive oil and garlic. Sauté the garlic, stirring, for 1 minute but don't let it color. Add the flour and cook, stirring, until the mixture begins to color, 8 to 10 minutes.

2. Gradually pour in the clam juice and Pernod and cook, stirring constantly, for 2 minutes. Add the tomatoes, parsley, bay leaf, and red pepper flakes. Simmer, stirring occasionally, for 5 minutes.

3. Place the ground-up pine nuts into a small bowl and add a few tablespoons of the broth to make a paste. Stir the paste back into the clam juice broth, and bring to a simmer over medium heat. Add the shrimp or scallops and simmer gently for 10 minutes. Add the fish and continue simmering for another 10 minutes. Taste and adjust the seasoning, and serve.

Leslie Revsin's Seafood Stew

I adapted this recipe from Leslie Revsin's wonderful book Great Fish, Quick. *The combination of shrimp, clams, mussels, scallops, and oysters is a great one, but feel free to replace any one of these ingredients with an equal amount of one of the others, or even some firm-fleshed fish. Serve with boiled potatoes and a salad.*

Serves 4

4 tablespoons butter
1 large onion, finely chopped
4 garlic cloves, finely chopped
1 red bell pepper, cored, seeded, and coarsely chopped
1 teaspoon *herbes de Provence* or a combination of some of the following:
    thyme, rosemary, basil, fennel seed, and marjoram
1 bay leaf
2 tablespoons flour
2 cups hot chicken broth
8 littleneck clams, scrubbed, rinsed, and drained
1 pound mussels, scrubbed, rinsed, and drained
$^1/_2$ pound shrimp, peeled
$^3/_4$ pound bay scallops or sea scallops, cut in half, rinsed, and dried on
    paper towels
1 dozen shucked oysters with their liquor
$^1/_4$ cup half-and-half or milk
Salt and freshly ground black pepper
2 tablespoons finely chopped fresh parsley

1. Put the butter in a large Dutch oven with a lid over medium-high heat. When the butter has melted add the onion, garlic, bell pepper, dried herbs, and bay leaf. Sauté, stirring frequently, for 10 minutes, until the onions are wilted. Reduce the heat to low and stir in the flour. Cook, stirring constantly, for 1 minute. Whisk in the hot chicken broth, raise the heat to medium-high, and bring to a boil, then reduce heat to a low simmer. The sauce will be rather thick at this point.

2. Add the clams to the sauce, cover the pot, and simmer over medium heat for 5 to 7 minutes, or until the clams begin to open. Add the mussels, stir, cover, and simmer for 2 minutes. (The stew will still be very thick at this point.) Add the shrimp and scallops, cover the pot, and simmer for another 2 minutes. Remove the cover and stir the stew. The clams and mussels should have started to open and release their juices into the stew. Cover and simmer for another 2 minutes, until the shrimp and scallops are cooked through. Add the oysters, with their liquor, cover, and cook 1 minute more.

3. Transfer the seafood to a warm, large serving bowl or to individual bowls. Pour the half-and-half or milk into a small saucepan and heat it through, then pour it into the sauce and stir well. Season to taste with salt and pepper. Pour over the seafood. Sprinkle with chopped parsley and serve.

Note

If the clams are not yet fully open when the rest of the seafood is cooked, remove the cooked seafood with a slotted spoon into a large serving bowl, or divide among individual bowls. Cover the pot with the clams in it and cook for another 3 to 5 minutes, until the clams have opened. Remove them with a slotted spoon and add to the seafood in the bowl(s). If there are still any unopened clams or mussels, remove them from the pot and discard them.

Monkfish Stewed in Red Wine

Fish stewed in red wine is no longer seen as unusual. In this stew, a good Burgundy and monkfish, which has a lobster-like texture, make for a wonderfully rich combination. Serve the stew with boiled or mashed potatoes. This recipe is adapted from The Modern Seafood Cook, *by Edward Brown and Arthur Boehm.*

Serves 4

> 4 tablespoons olive oil
> 2 pounds monkfish fillet, cut into 2-inch pieces
> 5 leeks, white and pale green parts only, washed and cut into 1-inch pieces
> 2 medium carrots, peeled and sliced $1/4$ inch thick
> 2 celery stalks, peeled and sliced $1/4$ inch thick
> 4 garlic cloves, finely minced or pushed through a garlic press
> 1 pound mushrooms, trimmed and quartered
> $3/4$ cup clam juice or fish stock
> 2 cups dry red wine
> 2 bay leaves
> 1 tablespoon fresh thyme leaves, or 1 teaspoon dried
> $1^1/2$ teaspoons cornstarch
> Salt and freshly ground black pepper

1. Place a Dutch oven or other stew-type pot over medium-high heat and add 2 tablespoons of the oil. When the oil starts to shimmer, add the monkfish in two batches and sauté until the fish is lightly colored on both sides. Transfer the fish to a warm platter.

2. Add the remaining oil to the pot, and when it is hot, add the leeks, carrots, celery, garlic, and mushrooms. Sauté, stirring, for 5 minutes, then add the clam juice, wine, bay leaves, and thyme. Bring to a boil, reduce the heat to medium-low, and simmer for 10 minutes, until the carrots are almost tender.

3. Return the monkfish to the pot and simmer over low heat for 10 to 12 minutes, until the fish is tender.

4. Put the cornstarch in a small bowl and stir in a tablespoon of the red wine sauce. Raise the heat under the stew to medium-high, stir in the starch mixture, and cook until the sauce has thickened a little, about 1 minute. Taste and adjust the seasonings and serve.

Monkfish and Scallop Stew with Corn and Tomatoes

This is a great stew for late summer when bay scallops come on the market, and fresh corn, ripe tomatoes, and fresh basil are at the farm stands. Serve in soup bowls with crusty bread.

Serves 6

1 pound monkfish
1 pound bay scallops, or sea scallops cut in half
$1/2$ cup all-purpose flour
$1/2$ teaspoon salt
$1/2$ teaspoon freshly ground black pepper
$1/4$ teaspoon cayenne
$1/2$ cup canola or vegetable oil
4 tablespoons unsalted butter
3 garlic cloves, finely minced or pushed through a garlic press
1 leek, finely sliced
$3/4$ cup dry white wine
$3/4$ cup fish stock or clam juice
$1 1/2$ cups fresh corn kernels (about 3 ears of corn)
2 large ripe tomatoes, peeled, seeded, and chopped (about $1 1/2$ cups)
$3/4$ cup fresh basil, finely shredded

1. Cut the monkfish into pieces roughly the size of scallops. In a small bowl, mix together the flour, salt, fresh black pepper, and cayenne. Dust the monkfish and scallops with the seasoned flour.

2. Heat the oil in a large skillet or sauté pan over medium-high heat and add the seafood in a single layer. Cook until the pieces turn golden brown, about 1½ minutes on each side. Drain on paper towels and finish cooking the rest of the fish and scallops.

3. Discard the cooking oil and wipe out the skillet. Add the butter and melt over medium-high heat until it starts to sizzle. Add the garlic and leek and cook over medium heat, stirring constantly, for about 1 minute. Do not let the garlic burn. Add the wine, increase the heat to high, and cook until the wine is reduced by half. Add the fish stock or clam juice, corn, tomatoes, and basil. Cook, stirring, for 5 minutes. Add the monkfish and scallops and heat through. Stir in the basil. Serve as soon as possible.

Quick Shrimp Curry

A quick and easy stew, this is a perfect dish for last-minute dinner guests, or for any evening when you would like to have a nice meal but don't have much time to prepare one. Serve it over rice, with a salad on the side.

Serves 4

> 2 tablespoons olive oil
> 1 large onion, finely chopped
> 4 garlic cloves, finely chopped
> 1 tablespoon Madras curry powder
> 1 cup clam juice
> 3 cups water
> 2 pounds shrimp, peeled
> 1 10-ounce package frozen peas, thawed
> 1/2 cup crème fraîche or plain yogurt
> 1/4 cup finely chopped fresh cilantro

1. Place the oil in a large skillet over medium-high heat. When the oil starts to shimmer, add the onion and garlic and sauté, stirring frequently, for 10 minutes, until the onion is wilted.
2. Reduce the heat to low and stir in the curry powder, cooking and stirring for 1 minute. Stir in the clam juice, raise the heat to medium-low, and cook for 10 minutes. Add 3 cups of water and simmer, stirring occasionally, until the sauce is slightly thickened, about 20 minutes.

3. Add the shrimp and cook over medium-high heat, stirring occasionally, for 2 minutes, or until the shrimp turn pink. Add the peas and crème fraîche or yogurt and simmer for 5 minutes until the peas are tender. Sprinkle with fresh cilantro and serve.

Shrimp and Feta Stew

This traditional Greek stew sounds like an unusual combination but actually works extremely well, with the cheese not only adding flavor but a great creamy quality as well. Serve with rice or good crusty bread.

Serves 4

1/4 cup olive oil
1 large onion, finely chopped
4 garlic cloves, finely chopped
3 cups chopped and drained canned tomatoes
1 cup dry white wine
1 tablespoon chopped fresh oregano, or 1 teaspoon dried
Salt and freshly ground black pepper
2 pounds large shrimp, peeled
1/3 pound feta cheese, drained and cut into 1/4-inch cubes
1/4 cup chopped flat-leafed parsley

1. Place the oil in a large skillet over medium-high heat. When the oil starts to shimmer, add the onion and garlic and sauté, stirring frequently, for 10 minutes, until the onion is wilted. Add the tomatoes, wine, and oregano and season with salt and pepper.
2. Raise heat to medium-high and bring to a boil. Reduce heat to medium and simmer, partially covered, for about 20 minutes until the sauce has reduced and thickened.
3. Add the shrimp and simmer, stirring occasionally, for 2 minutes, until the shrimp have turned pink. Stir in the cheese and parsley and serve.

Shrimp and Corn Stew

This type of corn stew is known as Maquechoux *in Louisiana. It can be prepared using only corn kernels and seasonings, or it can include seafood or chicken. It is a great summer meal when good sweet corn is fresh on the cobs, but it can also be prepared in another season, using good quality frozen corn kernels. Serve with crusty bread and a platter of sliced ripe tomatoes.*

Serves 4

3 tablespoons olive oil
1 large onion, finely chopped
2 medium green bell peppers, cored, seeded, and diced
1 large red bell pepper, cored, seeded, and diced
1 large jalapeño pepper, cored, seeded, and diced
1^1/$_2$ pounds medium shrimp, peeled and deveined
3^1/$_2$ to 4 cups fresh corn kernels from 6 ears shucked corn
1 cup chicken stock
^{1}/$_2$ cup chopped fresh parsley
^{1}/$_2$ teaspoon freshly ground black pepper
^{1}/$_4$ teaspoon cayenne
Dash of Tabasco or other hot pepper sauce
Salt to taste

1. In a large deep-sided skillet, heat the oil over medium-high heat. Add the onion and all the peppers and sauté until softened, about

10 minutes. Add the shrimp, and cook, stirring, until it turns pink, about 5 minutes.

2. Add the corn, chicken stock, parsley, black pepper, cayenne, hot sauce, and salt to taste. Cook over high heat until heated through. Taste and adjust the seasonings and serve.

Shrimp in Green Chili Sauce with Beans

Green chilies and shrimp make for a great combination, and the wonderful thing about this recipe is that once you have peeled the shrimp, the dish takes only half an hour to prepare. Serve it over buttered rice.

Serves 6

2 tablespoons olive oil

1 tablespoon unsalted butter

1 large white onion, finely chopped

6 garlic cloves, finely chopped

2 tablespoons all-purpose flour

1½ to 2 cups roasted and peeled mild green chilies, fresh, frozen, or canned, coarsely chopped

2 large ripe tomatoes, finely chopped, or 1 cup drained and coarsely chopped canned tomatoes

1 teaspoon dried Mexican oregano, crushed between your fingers

½ teaspoon ground cumin

2 to 3 cups hot chicken broth, or part clam broth

2 pounds medium shrimp, peeled and deveined

1 15-ounce can of white beans, drained and rinsed

Salt

Tabasco or other hot pepper sauce

½ cup finely chopped fresh cilantro

1. Heat the oil and butter in a large skillet or sauté pan over medium-high heat until the butter starts to foam. Add the onion and cook, stirring, until it softens, about 5 minutes. Add the garlic and cook, stirring, 3 minutes longer.
2. Sprinkle the flour over the onion and cook, stirring, for 5 minutes longer to make a roux. Add the chilies, tomatoes, oregano, and cumin. Cook, stirring, for 3 minutes.
3. Stir in 2 cups of chicken broth, add the shrimp and beans, stir, and simmer over medium heat for 10 to 15 minutes until the shrimp are pink and cooked through. Add more chicken broth to achieve the desired consistency. I like it fairly soupy so that there's lots of sauce; other people like it thicker with less liquid.
4. Taste for seasoning and add salt and hot sauce to taste. Sprinkle with cilantro and serve.

Note
Tabasco's new green jalapeño sauce is particularly delicious with this chili.

Seafood, Sausage, and Chicken Gumbo

This recipe is adapted from one of my favorite old books, called Creole Gumbo and All That Jazz, *by Howard Mitcham. It is also one of the best gumbo recipes I know. Serve over rice, with crusty bread and a salad.*

Serves 8 to 10

1 3-pound chicken, cut into 8 pieces, all visible fat removed
1 teaspoon salt
$1/2$ teaspoon dried thyme
1 bay leaf
2 pounds medium shrimp
$1/2$ cup canola or vegetable oil
$1/2$ cup flour
2 large onions, finely chopped
4 garlic cloves, finely chopped
2 stalks of celery, finely chopped
1 green bell pepper, cored, seeded, and finely chopped
4 scallions, green parts included, finely chopped
1 pound andouille sausage or smoked Polish kielbasa, cut in half
    lengthwise and cut crosswise into $1/2$-inch pieces
$1/4$ teaspoon cayenne
3 dozen shucked oysters and their liquor
Salt and freshly ground black pepper

1. Place the cut-up chicken pieces in a medium-large pot together with the salt, thyme, and bay leaf. Add enough cold water to cover the chicken, bring to a boil, reduce heat to medium-low, and simmer, partially covered, for 45 minutes.

2. Remove the chicken pieces to a plate and skim as much fat as possible from the broth. When the chicken is cool enough to handle, remove the skin from the meat and the meat from the bones. Pull the meat apart into small pieces, and set it aside. Discard the skin and bones.

3. Place the shrimp in another pot, cover with cold water, and add $\frac{1}{2}$ teaspoon of salt. Bring to a boil over medium-high heat, and continue boiling for 5 minutes. Remove the shrimp from the pot, keeping the liquid. Peel the shrimp, reserving the shells, but do not devein them and set aside. Return the shells to the shrimp broth in the pot and boil vigorously for 15 minutes. Strain the broth and discard the shrimp shells. Add the shrimp broth to the chicken broth.

4. Place the oil in a large Dutch oven over low heat. Slowly stir in the flour and keep stirring until the mixture is creamy and has no lumps. Turn the heat very low and keep stirring, scraping up from the bottom, until the roux turns a medium brown color, about 20 minutes.

5. Add the onions, garlic, celery, bell pepper, and scallions and cook, stirring, over medium-low heat until the vegetables are soft and translucent, 10 to 15 minutes. Add the chicken, sausage, cayenne,

and enough of the chicken-shrimp broth to cover by 1 inch. Add water or chicken broth, if necessary. Simmer over medium-low heat for 1 hour.

6. Add the shrimp, oysters, and oyster liquor and cook 10 minutes longer. Remove from heat and taste for seasoning, adding salt and pepper to taste.

three

Chicken Stews

Chicken with Riesling Wine

Here is a lovely recipe adapted from a classic Alsatian dish, Coq au Riesling, *which is served throughout the French region of Alsace-Lorraine. It is often made richer with the addition of egg yolks at the end, but I prefer to keep this recipe simple. I like to serve this stew with a salad of Belgian endives and some crispy bread.*

Serves 4

$3^{1}/_{2}$- to 4-pound chicken, cut into small serving pieces, or $3^{1}/_{2}$ to 4 pounds chicken legs and thighs, skin and visible fat removed

Salt and freshly ground black pepper

2 tablespoons unsalted butter

2 tablespoons olive oil

2 large onions, finely chopped

2 carrots, peeled and cut into $^{1}/_{2}$-inch pieces

$^{1}/_{2}$ pound fresh mushrooms, trimmed and quartered

1 tablespoon fresh thyme leaves, or 1 teaspoon dried

1 bay leaf

1 cup Riesling

$^{2}/_{3}$ cup heavy cream

1. Rinse the chicken under cold running water and dry on paper towels. Sprinkle the chicken pieces with salt and pepper.
2. Place 1 tablespoon of the butter and 1 tablespoon of the olive oil in a large skillet over medium-high heat and when the butter has melted, add the chicken pieces in batches so that they do not

43

crowd each other. Lightly brown the chicken pieces on all sides and remove them to a platter.

3. Add the remaining butter and oil to the skillet and place over medium-high heat. When the butter has melted add the onions, carrots, and mushrooms and sauté, stirring frequently, for 10 minutes, until the onions have wilted and the mushrooms have released their juices.

4. Return the chicken pieces, along with any juices, to the skillet. Add the thyme, bay leaf, and Riesling. Reduce heat to low, cover the skillet, and simmer for 30 minutes, until the chicken pieces are tender.

5. Use a slotted spoon to remove the chicken and mushrooms to a warm serving dish. Increase heat under the skillet to high and boil the liquid until it reduces by half, about 10 minutes. Add the cream to the skillet and cook, stirring, until the sauce thickens a little. Taste and adjust the seasonings as necessary, pour over the chicken, and serve.

Chicken Cacciatore

This classic dish is popular in both Italy and America. It is easy to make and works well year round but is especially delicious in the summer and fall, when good vine-ripe tomatoes are available, as well as fresh rosemary and basil. Serve with some Italian bread.

Serves 6

4 pounds chicken legs and thighs, skin and visible fat removed, or a
    4-pound roasting chicken, cut into serving pieces
Salt and freshly ground black pepper
$1/4$ cup olive oil
4 medium-size onions, finely chopped
2 garlic cloves, finely chopped
1 cup dry white wine
$1^1/2$ cups chopped canned or "fresh pack" tomatoes, or 1 pound vine-ripe
    tomatoes, peeled and chopped
2 tablespoons finely chopped fresh rosemary leaves
2 bay leaves
Finely chopped fresh basil leaves

1. Wash the chicken pieces under cold running water and dry on paper towels. Sprinkle the pieces with salt and pepper.
2. Place 2 tablespoons of the oil in a large skillet over medium-high heat and when the oil starts to shimmer, add the chicken pieces in batches so that they do not crowd each other. Brown the chicken pieces on all sides and remove them to a platter.

3. Add the remaining 2 tablespoons of olive oil to the skillet and add the chopped onions and garlic. Cook over medium-high heat, stirring, until the onions have softened, about 10 minutes.
4. Add the chicken pieces, the wine, tomatoes, rosemary, and bay leaves. Cover and cook over medium heat for 45 minutes, or until the chicken is tender.
5. Taste for seasoning and add more salt and pepper if necessary. Sprinkle with basil leaves just before serving.

Variations

1. Add some Parmesan rind at step 4 and cook it with the chicken until it is done. The rind will provide a great deal of flavor to the stew.
2. Stir in some sautéed shiitake mushroom caps to the stew at step 4 to impart a great woodsy flavor.

Chicken Paprikash

The sweet paprika and the sour cream are what make this a traditional Hungarian dish. It is easy to prepare and will be very popular with your guests. Serve with bread and a salad.

Serves 6

$4^{1}/_2$ to 5 pounds chicken legs and thighs, skin and visible fat removed
2 small onions, finely chopped
5 garlic cloves, finely chopped
$^{1}/_4$ cup chopped fresh dill
2 cups chicken broth
1 cup dry white wine
$^{1}/_4$ cup sweet paprika
$^{1}/_4$ cup tomato puree
$^{3}/_4$ cup sour cream

1. Preheat the oven to 300° F.
2. Rinse the chicken under cold running water and dry on paper towels. Place the chicken in a large wide saucepan and add the onions, garlic, 2 tablespoons of the dill, chicken broth, and wine. Bring to a boil over high heat, reduce the heat to medium-low, and simmer, uncovered, for 20 minutes.
3. Remove the chicken pieces to a baking pan and place in the oven while you prepare the sauce.
4. Skim away as much fat as possible from the stock in the pan, place over high heat, and cook until the liquid is reduced by half,

about 15 minutes. Stir in the paprika and the tomato puree and continue to cook until the sauce thickens slightly, about 10 minutes. Remove from the heat and stir in the sour cream. Taste for seasoning and add salt if necessary.

5. Return the chicken to the sauce, sprinkle with the remaining dill, and serve.

Chicken with Wine and Prunes

This recipe is based on Mark Bittman's recipe for Coq au Vin with Prunes, which appeared in the New York Times *on January 30, 2002. He simplifies the classic recipe for Coq au Vin, and with the addition of prunes, adds a delightful sweetness and depth of flavor.*

Serves 4

> $2^1/2$ to 3 pounds chicken legs and thighs, visible fat removed, or 1 3-pound chicken cut into serving pieces, skin and fat removed
> Salt and freshly ground black pepper
> 2 tablespoons olive oil
> 2 large onions, finely chopped
> 4 garlic cloves, finely chopped
> 2 cups dry red wine
> 1 pound pitted prunes
> 1 tablespoon unsalted butter
> $1/4$ cup finely chopped fresh parsley, for garnish

1. Wash the chicken pieces under cold running water and dry on paper towels. Sprinkle the pieces with salt and pepper.
2. Place the oil in a large skillet over medium heat and when the oil starts to shimmer, add the chicken pieces in batches so that they do not crowd each other. Brown the chicken pieces on all sides and remove them to a large Dutch oven with a lid.

3. Add the onions and garlic to the skillet. Cook over medium-high heat, stirring, until the onions have softened, about 10 minutes. Transfer them to the Dutch oven.

4. Turn the heat under the skillet to medium-high and add 1 cup of the wine. Cook, stirring frequently with a wooden spoon to scrape up any browned bits from the bottom of the skillet, until the wine is reduced by half. Pour the wine into the Dutch oven and add the remaining 1 cup of wine and the prunes.

5. Place the Dutch oven over medium-high heat and bring the stew to a boil. Reduce heat to low and cover the pan. Simmer gently for 30 minutes, until the chicken is tender. Remove the lid, stir in the butter, and sprinkle with parsley. Remove from the heat and serve.

Chicken Stew Bouillabaisse-Style

This is a soupy stew with all the flavor of a fish bouillabaisse, but with chicken as the main ingredient. I've come across many versions of this recipe, but the best one I found was in Bistro Cooking *by Patricia Wells. This is my version of her recipe. You will need to marinate the chicken the day before you prepare the dish.*

Serves 4

4 fennel bulbs with fronds, coarsely chopped

2 large onions, coarsely chopped

2 cups drained and chopped canned or "fresh pack" tomatoes

6 garlic cloves, peeled and crushed

1/3 cup Pernod

3 tablespoons olive oil

Pinch of saffron threads

2 tablespoons finely chopped fresh thyme, or 2 teaspoons dried

4 bay leaves

Salt and freshly ground black pepper

1/8 to 1/4 teaspoon cayenne

4 chicken thighs and 4 drumsticks, skin and visible fat removed, rinsed
    under cold water, and dried

1 pound baby Yukon Gold or red-skinned potatoes, peeled and quartered

2 cups chicken broth

1. In a large Dutch oven combine the fennel, onions, tomatoes, garlic, Pernod, olive oil, saffron, thyme, bay leaves, salt, pepper, and cayenne. Mix well, add the chicken thighs and drumsticks, and mix again. Cover and refrigerate for 8 to 12 hours.

2. Remove the Dutch oven with the chicken from the refrigerator at least 1 hour before starting to cook. When the chicken reaches room temperature, place the Dutch oven over medium-high heat and bring to a boil. Reduce the heat to medium-low, cover, and simmer, stirring occasionally, for 30 minutes. Add the potatoes and chicken broth and continue to simmer gently for 30 to 45 minutes, until the potatoes are cooked through and the chicken pieces are tender.

Chicken Stew with Apple Cider and Parsnips

Apple cider, parsnips, and carrots add elegant notes of sweetness to this easy-to-make chicken stew. It makes a perfect winter dish when other vegetables are hard to find. Serve with egg noodles or rice to catch the delicious sauce.

Serves 4

$2^1/2$ to 3 pounds chicken legs and thighs
Salt and freshly ground black pepper
2 tablespoons olive oil
1 tablespoon flour, preferably Wondra
1 cup apple cider
$1^1/2$ cups chicken broth
1 large onion, cut in half lengthwise and thinly sliced
1 pound parsnips, peeled and cut into 1-inch pieces
3 large carrots, peeled and cut into 1-inch pieces
1 tablespoon fresh thyme leaves, or 1 teaspoon dried

1. Preheat the oven to 400° F.
2. Rinse the chicken pieces under cold running water and dry on paper towels.
3. Place the oil in a large oven-proof skillet over medium-high heat and add the chicken pieces in batches so that they do not crowd each other. Brown the chicken pieces on all sides and remove them to a platter.

53

4. Discard all but 1 tablespoon of fat from the pot. Reduce heat to medium and stir in the flour, stirring for 1 minute. Whisk in the apple cider and the chicken broth and bring to a simmer. Stir frequently to scrape up any browned bits from the bottom. Add the onion, parsnips, carrots, and thyme and return the chicken pieces to the skillet. Bring the stew to a simmer, cover, and place in the oven for 20 to 25 minutes, until the chicken and vegetables are tender. Season with salt and pepper and serve.

Moroccan Chicken Stew with Apples

You can make this simple recipe using apples, pears, fresh dates, or quinces, or a combination of any of them. You can also use dried fruit— apricots, prunes, pears, or raisins. Any or all of these ingredients will make for a delicious, simple stew. Serve this stew with rice or couscous.

Serves 6

> 4 to 4$^{1}/_{2}$ pounds chicken legs and thighs, skin and visible fat removed
> 2 large onions, finely chopped
> $^{1}/_{4}$ cup finely chopped fresh parsley
> 3 tablespoons unsalted butter
> $^{1}/_{4}$ teaspoon ground ginger
> Salt and freshly ground black pepper
> 1 pound crisp, fresh eating apples, peeled, cored, and sliced
> $^{1}/_{4}$ cup golden raisins

1. Rinse the chicken pieces under cold running water and dry on paper towels. Put the chicken pieces into a large pot, together with the onion, parsley, butter, ginger, salt, and pepper. Add enough cold water to just cover the chicken. Bring to a boil over medium-high heat, reduce heat to medium-low, and simmer, partially covered, for 1 hour, until the chicken is very tender and the liquid has been reduced almost by half.

2. Add the sliced apples and raisins and simmer over low heat for about 10 minutes, until the apples are just tender.

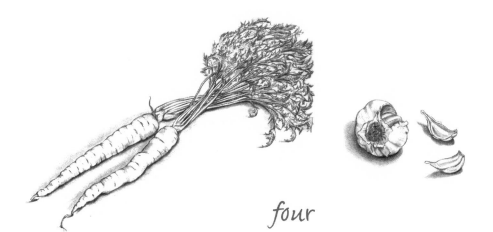

four

Veal Stews

Blanquette de Veau

This is a classic, ancient French veal stew that is easy to prepare and very satisfying to eat. The meat here is never browned but is simmered in a stock with herbs and vegetables. At the end the sauce is enriched with cream and egg yolks. Serve with noodles or mashed potatoes.

Serves 6 to 8

4 pounds boned leg of veal, cut into 1½-inch cubes

5 cups chicken broth

2 cups white wine

A bouquet garni tied in a cheesecloth: 1 celery stalk without leaves, 10 parsley stems, 2 bay leaves, 1 sprig of thyme, 2 cloves, and 10 peppercorns

2 large carrots, cut into 2-inch pieces

1 large onion, quartered

½ cup of stock dipped from the simmering veal

5 tablespoons unsalted butter

1 10-ounce package of small frozen onions, thawed

Salt and freshly ground black pepper

5 tablespoons all-purpose flour

1 pound small white mushrooms, stems trimmed off and discarded

1 to 2 tablespoons fresh lemon juice

3 large egg yolks at room temperature

½ cup heavy cream at room temperature

2 tablespoons finely chopped fresh tarragon or parsley

1. Place the veal cubes in an enameled Dutch oven with enough cold water to cover by 2 inches. Bring to a boil over high heat,

skimming away as much scum as possible. Drain the meat in a colander and rinse it under cold running water to remove any remnants of scum.

2. Return the meat to the Dutch oven and add the chicken broth, wine, bouquet garni, carrots, and onion. Turn the heat to medium-high, partially cover the pot, and bring to a simmer. Reduce the heat to low and continue to simmer gently, partially covered, for 1½ hours, until the veal is tender.

3. While the meat is simmering, add ½ cup of stock from the simmering veal to a small saucepan, together with 1 tablespoon of the butter and the frozen onions. Season to taste with salt and pepper and simmer over low heat for 30 to 40 minutes. Remove from the heat and set aside.

4. When the veal has finished cooking, pour the stew into a colander set over a bowl. Drain the meat, discard the bouquet garni, transfer the meat to a bowl, and keep it warm. Return the broth to the Dutch oven and turn the heat to high. Boil the broth until it is reduced to 3½ to 4 cups.

5. In a medium-size saucepan, melt the remaining 4 tablespoons of butter over low heat. Stir in the flour and keep stirring until the butter-flour combination starts to foam. Remove from the heat and gradually whisk in the broth from the stew. Return it to the stove, place over high heat, and bring the broth to a boil. Reduce the heat to low and simmer for 10 minutes, skimming the surface frequently. Stir in the onions and the mushroom caps and simmer

for another 10 minutes, still skimming the surface. Taste the sauce and season with salt, pepper, and fresh lemon juice.

6. Pour the sauce and vegetables over the veal and pour a little bit of stock (2 tablespoons) over the top to prevent a skin from forming. (The stew may be done a day ahead at this point. Cover and refrigerate.)

7. Place the veal stew over medium-low heat and bring to a simmer. Simmer gently for 5 to 10 minutes and remove from the heat. Whisk the egg yolks and cream together in a medium-size bowl. Scoop out 1 cup of hot sauce from the stew and whisk it in, a few spoonfuls at a time. Pour the egg yolk mixture gradually into the stew, stirring frequently to mix everything together. Set over medium-low heat for a few minutes, until the entire sauce has thickened slightly, but do not let it come to a boil! Remove from heat, garnish with tarragon or parsley, and serve immediately.

Veal Stew Marengo

This classic Marengo stew, which can also be made with chicken instead of veal, is said to have been invented by Napoleon's chef after the Battle of Marengo. Serve it with noodles or boiled potatoes.

Serves 4 to 6

3 pounds boned leg of veal, cut into $1^1/_2$-inch cubes
Salt and freshly ground black pepper
2 tablespoons flour, preferably Wondra
3 tablespoons olive oil
1 medium-size onion, finely chopped
3 garlic cloves, finely chopped
$1^1/_2$ cups dry white wine or dry vermouth
2 cups drained and chopped canned tomatoes
1 teaspoon fresh thyme leaves, or $^1/_2$ teaspoon dried
1 teaspoon finely chopped fresh tarragon, or $^1/_2$ teaspoon dried
1 3-inch strip of orange peel
2 tablespoons butter
1 pound fresh white button or porcini mushroom caps, cut in half

1. Preheat the oven to 350° F.
2. Dry the veal cubes on paper towels. Sprinkle with salt, pepper, and flour. Place 2 tablespoons of the olive oil in a large heavy skillet over medium-high heat and when the oil starts to shimmer, add the veal cubes in batches so that they do not crowd each other. Brown the cubes on one or two sides and remove them to a large enameled Dutch oven with a lid.

3. Add the remaining 1 tablespoon of olive oil with the onion and garlic to the skillet and sauté over medium-high heat, stirring frequently with a wooden spoon to scrape up any browned bits from the bottom of the skillet. When the onion has wilted, about 10 minutes, add the wine to the skillet and cook, stirring, for 1 minute. Pour the wine and onion into the Dutch oven and stir to mix with the veal cubes; then add the tomatoes, thyme, tarragon, and orange peel.

4. Cover the Dutch oven and place it into the preheated oven for 1 hour.

5. Melt the butter in a skillet over medium-high heat, add the mushrooms, season with salt and pepper, and sauté for 5 to 6 minutes. Add the mushrooms to the stew after it has cooked for 1 hour. Return to the oven and cook for 20 to 30 minutes longer, until the meat is very tender. Remove from the oven and serve.

Veal Stew with Fennel and Mustard

Here's a very easy stew with great flavors that come from fennel and mustard.

Serves 6

2¹/₂ pounds boned leg of veal, cut into 1¹/₂-inch cubes
Salt and freshly ground black pepper
3 tablespoons olive oil
3 heads of fennel, stalks and fronds removed, each head cut in half and thinly sliced
6 medium carrots, peeled and cut into 2-inch lengths
1 cup chicken broth
1 cup dry white wine or dry vermouth
3 tablespoons Dijon mustard
3 tablespoons heavy cream or sour cream
¹/₂ cup finely chopped flat-leaf parsley

1. Dry the veal cubes on paper towels. Sprinkle with salt and pepper. Place the 2 tablespoons of oil in a large heavy skillet over medium-high heat and when the oil starts to shimmer, add the veal cubes in batches so that they do not crowd each other. Brown the cubes on one or two sides and remove them to an enameled Dutch oven with a lid.
2. Add the remaining olive oil, fennel, and carrots and sauté over medium-high heat, stirring frequently with a wooden spoon to

scrape up any browned bits from the bottom of the skillet. When the fennel has browned on one side, about 5 minutes, turn the fennel and brown the other side, about 3 minutes. Add the broth and wine to the skillet and cook, stirring, for 1 minute. Pour the vegetables and broth into the Dutch oven and stir to mix with the veal cubes.

3. Bring the stew to a simmer over medium-high heat, reduce heat to low, and simmer partially covered for $1\frac{1}{2}$ hours, stirring occasionally, until meat is very tender. Pour the stew into a colander set over a bowl. Return the broth to the Dutch oven. Blend the mustard and cream in a small bowl, then whisk the mustard-cream mixture into the sauce until it is all smooth. Return the meat and vegetables to the Dutch oven and heat through, if necessary. Garnish with parsley and serve.

Spring Veal Ragout

This veal stew with asparagus and peas is a perfect meal for a cool spring evening. Serve it over noodles or rice.

Serves 4

    2 pounds veal stew meat, cut into 1¹/₂-inch cubes
    Salt and freshly ground black pepper
    ¹/₄ cup flour, preferably Wondra
    2 tablespoons olive oil
    6 scallions, white and green parts sliced separately
    1 cup dry white wine
    1 cup chicken broth
    1 tablespoon chopped fresh tarragon, or 1 teaspoon dried
    8 ounces baby carrots
    ¹/₂ pound new potatoes, scrubbed and cubed
    1 pound asparagus, peeled and cut into 2-inch pieces
    1 cup fresh or frozen peas
    1 teaspoon freshly grated lemon zest

1. Dry the veal cubes on paper towels. Sprinkle with salt, pepper, and flour. Place 2 tablespoons of oil in a large heavy skillet over medium-high heat and when the oil starts to shimmer, add the veal cubes in batches so that they do not crowd each other. Brown the cubes on one or two sides and remove them to a plate.
2. Add the sliced white scallion parts to the pan and cook, stirring for 2 minutes.

3. Add the wine to the skillet and cook, stirring with a wooden spoon to scrape up any browned bits from the bottom. Cook until the wine is reduced by half. Return the veal cubes and any juices to the skillet. Add the chicken broth and half the fresh tarragon or all of the dried and bring to a boil. Reduce heat to low and simmer, covered, for 1 hour.

4. Add the carrots and potatoes and continue cooking for 20 minutes. Add the asparagus, peas, the rest of the fresh tarragon, and lemon zest. Simmer for another 10 minutes, until all the vegetables are tender. Season to taste with salt and pepper. Sprinkle with chopped green scallions and serve.

Veal Stew with Carrots, Parsnips, and Potatoes

Serve this hearty stew with a crusty French bread and a salad.

Serves 6

> 3 pounds boned leg of veal, cut into 2-inch cubes
> Salt and freshly ground black pepper
> 3 tablespoons olive oil
> 3 medium-size onions, cut in half and sliced
> 6 garlic cloves, finely chopped
> 2 cups chicken broth
> 1/2 cup dry white wine or dry vermouth
> 1 bay leaf
> 6 medium carrots, peeled and cut into 1-inch pieces
> 4 large parsnips, peeled, cut in half lengthwise, and cut into 1-inch pieces
> 4 medium-size red-skinned potatoes, peeled and cubed
> 3 tablespoons chopped fresh sage

1. Dry the veal cubes on paper towels and sprinkle them with salt and pepper. Place 2 tablespoons of the olive oil in a large heavy skillet over medium-high heat and when the oil starts to shimmer, add the veal cubes in batches so that they do not crowd each other. Brown the cubes on one or two sides and remove them to a large enameled Dutch oven with a lid.

2. Heat the remaining tablespoon of oil in the same skillet and add onions and garlic. Sauté over medium-high heat, stirring

frequently with a wooden spoon to scrape up any browned bits from the bottom of the skillet. When the onions have wilted, about 5 minutes, add the broth and wine to the skillet and cook, stirring, for 1 minute. Pour the broth and onions into the Dutch oven and stir to mix with the veal cubes. Add the bay leaf.

3. Place the Dutch oven over medium-high heat and bring to a boil. Reduce the heat to low, cover, and simmer for 1 hour. Add the carrots, parsnips, and potatoes, cover, and simmer for 20 minutes, until the potatoes are almost tender. Uncover and simmer for another 20 minutes, until the meat is very tender and the liquid has reduced to a saucy consistency.

4. Sprinkle with fresh sage and serve.

Veal Stew with Olives, Anchovies, and Basil

Here is a Mediterranean-inspired veal stew full of the sunny flavors of olives and basil. The anchovies add a rich, deep, but unrecognizable flavor, so if you don't mention them to your guests, they will never know they're in there. Serve with a crusty bread and a salad.

Serves 6

3 pounds boned leg of veal, cut into 2-inch cubes
Salt and freshly ground black pepper
$^1/_2$ cup flour, preferably Wondra
3 tablespoons olive oil
1 large onion, finely chopped
4 garlic cloves, finely chopped
1 cup dry red wine
2 cups drained and chopped canned tomatoes
1 cup pitted Kalamata olives, roughly chopped
20 basil leaves, roughly chopped
2 tablespoons chopped fresh flat-leaf parsley
2 teaspoons chopped fresh oregano, or 1 teaspoon dried
1 2-ounce can oil-packed anchovy fillets, drained, rinsed under hot water, and finely chopped
Additional basil for garnish

1. Preheat the oven to 325° F.

2. Dry the veal cubes on paper towels. Sprinkle with salt, pepper, and flour. Place the 2 tablespoons of the oil in a large heavy skillet over medium-high heat and when the oil starts to shimmer, add the lamb cubes in batches so that they do not crowd each other. Brown the cubes on one or two sides and remove them to a large Dutch oven with a lid.

3. Add the remaining olive oil, onion, and garlic to the skillet and sauté over medium-high heat, stirring frequently with a wooden spoon to scrape up any browned bits from the bottom of the skillet. When the onion has wilted, about 10 minutes, add the wine to the skillet and cook, stirring, for 1 minute. Pour the wine and onion into the Dutch oven and stir to mix with the veal cubes. Add the tomatoes, olives, basil, parsley, and oregano and stir.

4. Cover the Dutch oven and place it into the preheated oven for 1 hour.

5. Remove from the oven, stir in the anchovies, and continue to bake, covered, for 1 more hour, until the meat is very tender. Remove from the oven; garnish with basil and serve.

Veal and Sausage Stew with Beans and Spinach

This hearty stew is definitely a "meal in a bowl" and requires nothing more than a good crusty bread and a nice glass of wine to go with it.

Serves 6

> 1 pound veal stew meat, cut into 1-inch cubes
> Salt and freshly ground black pepper
> 1 pound Italian hot or sweet sausage, cut into 1-inch lengths
> 2 tablespoons olive oil
> 2 large onions, finely chopped
> 6 garlic cloves, finely minced or pushed through a garlic press
> 1 cup diced canned tomatoes, with juice
> 2 cups dry white wine
> 1 cup chicken broth
> 1 15-ounce can white cannellini beans, rinsed and drained
> 1 pound spinach, washed and dried
> 2 tablespoons freshly squeezed lemon juice

1. Dry the veal cubes on paper towels. Sprinkle with salt and pepper. Place the olive oil in a large heavy skillet over medium-high heat and when the oil starts to shimmer, add the veal cubes and sausages in batches so that they do not crowd each other. Brown the cubes on one or two sides and remove them to a large enameled Dutch oven with a lid.

73

2. Remove all but 2 tablespoons of fat from the pan. Add the onions and garlic and sauté over medium heat for 5 minutes, until the onions become translucent.

3. Transfer the onions to the Dutch oven and add the tomatoes, wine, and chicken broth. Bring to a boil, reduce heat to low, cover, and simmer until the meat is tender, 1 to 1½ hours. Stir in the beans and spinach, cover, and simmer for 10 to 15 minutes, until the spinach has wilted and cooked through. Stir in the lemon juice, season to taste with salt and pepper, and serve.

five

Beef Stews

Alsatian Beef, Lamb, and Pork Stew

Known locally as Baekeoffe,* *this Alsatian stew is a delicious combination of 3 different meats, along with potatoes, onions, and leeks. It is a classic meat-and-potatoes stew, suitable for any occasion. Serve with crispy bread and a green salad. Any leftovers make a perfect meal for the following day. The stew meat should marinate for 12 to 24 hours, so be sure to leave yourself enough time when preparing this dish.*

Serves 6 to 8

1 pound boneless beef stew meat, cut into 2-inch pieces
1 pound boneless lamb stew meat, cut into 2-inch pieces
1 pound boneless pork, cut into 2-inch pieces
4 carrots, peeled and thinly sliced
3 large onions, cut in half and thinly sliced
3 large leeks, white and pale green parts only, washed and thinly sliced
6 garlic cloves, peeled and crushed
Salt and freshly ground black pepper
10 fresh thyme sprigs, or 2 tablespoons dried thyme
10 parsley stems
3 bay leaves
1 bottle Alsatian white wine, such as Riesling or pinot blanc

Baekeoffe means baker's oven. Originally this dish was prepared on Mondays, when housewives usually did their laundry and had little time to cook. They brought the marinated stews to the local baker, who placed it into his wood-burning oven. When it was time for the midday meal, the stew was ready and brought home.

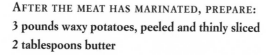

AFTER THE MEAT HAS MARINATED, PREPARE:
3 pounds waxy potatoes, peeled and thinly sliced
2 tablespoons butter

1. The day before you cook this stew, the meats should be marinated. Place the meats in a large nonreactive bowl with the carrots, onions, leeks, and garlic cloves. Season with salt and pepper.

2. Tie the thyme sprigs and the parsley stems together and add to the meats, along with the bay leaves and white wine. Mix well, cover, and refrigerate for 12 to 24 hours.

3. When you are ready to cook the meats, preheat the oven to 375° F.

4. Butter the inside of an enameled Dutch oven and add one-third of the potatoes to the bottom. Using a slotted spoon, add half the meat and vegetables to the Dutch oven. Cover with another third of the potatoes, then add the remaining meat and vegetables, and cover with the remaining potatoes. Pour the remaining wine and herbs over the meat mixture. Cover and bake for 3 hours, until the meats are very tender.

5. Bring the Dutch oven to the table and serve.

Stifado

This Greek stew (pronounced stifatho*) should have three times as many onions as beef. In fact, in Greek the name of the recipe implies that it is onion stew with beef. It requires a very long, slow cooking time and therefore is perfect for making in a slow cooker. It is an absolutely delicious dish, and the final additions of walnuts and feta cheese make it even tastier. Serve with crusty bread and a salad.*

Serves 4

> 1$^1/_2$ pounds lean beef chuck or flank steak, cut into narrow strips about
> $^1/_2$ inch wide and 2 inches long
> 3 tablespoons fresh lemon juice
> $^1/_4$ cup olive oil
> Salt and freshly ground black pepper
> 4$^1/_2$ to 5 pounds large yellow onions, cut in half and thickly sliced
> 6 garlic cloves, finely chopped
> 2 cups chopped canned tomatoes
> 2 tablespoons chopped fresh rosemary, or 1 teaspoon dried
> 2 tablespoons fresh thyme leaves, or 1 teaspoon dried
> 2 tablespoons chopped fresh oregano, or 1 teaspoon dried
> 1 cup dry red wine
> $^1/_2$ cup chopped toasted walnuts
> $^1/_2$ pound feta cheese, drained and crumbled

1. Put the beef slices in a medium-size bowl, pour the lemon juice over the beef, and toss with your hand to make sure that every piece is coated with lemon juice.

2. Heat the olive oil in a large Dutch oven with a tight-fitting lid and add the beef. Sauté over high heat, stirring constantly, until the meat is browned. Season with salt and pepper. Add the onions, garlic, tomatoes, rosemary, thyme, oregano, and wine. Stir well, place over very low heat, cover the pot, and simmer for 3 hours.

3. Remove the lid, stir the stew, and taste for seasoning, adding more salt and pepper if necessary. Replace the lid and simmer over very low heat for 1 hour longer, until most of the liquid has evaporated. Add the walnuts and feta cheese and simmer for 5 minutes.

Beef Stew with White Wine and Mustard

Most stews are thought of as being perfect winter dishes, but there are definitely some that cross that line, including this one. Inspired by one dubbed a daube by Patricia Wells in her book At Home in Provence, *this stew has a lightness that makes it work just as well in spring or even summer. Serve with noodles and a green vegetable on the side.*

Serves 8

> 4 pounds boneless beef chuck, cut into 2-inch cubes
> Salt and freshly ground black pepper
> 3 tablespoons olive oil
> 1 bottle dry white wine
> 1/4 cup Dijon mustard
> 3 cups peeled and halved plum tomatoes, with their juice
> 3 large onions, cut in half and thinly sliced
> 4 garlic cloves, peeled and crushed
> 2 bay leaves
> 1/3 cup chopped flat-leafed parsley
> 2 tablespoons finely chopped fresh tarragon, or 1 teaspoon dried
> 1 tablespoon fresh thyme leaves, or 1 teaspoons dried

1. Dry the beef cubes with paper towels and sprinkle with salt and pepper. Place the oil in a large heavy skillet over medium-high heat and when the oil starts to shimmer, add the beef cubes in

batches so that they do not crowd each other. Brown the cubes on all sides and remove them to a large Dutch oven with a lid.

2. Pour off any excess fat from the skillet and place it over medium-high heat. Add the wine and stir with a wooden spoon to scrape up any browned bits from the bottom. Reduce the heat to medium and simmer the wine until it is reduced by two-thirds, about 10 minutes. Turn off the heat and whisk in the mustard. Transfer to the Dutch oven.

3. Add the tomatoes with their juice, the onions, garlic, bay leaves, parsley, tarragon, and thyme. Place over low heat and simmer, covered, for 2 to 3 hours, until the beef is very tender. If the stew seems to liquid, remove the beef with a slotted spoon to a platter. Boil the sauce over high heat until reduced by about one-third. Return the beef and reheat gently.

Flemish Beef Stew with Beer

In Belgium this classic stew has two names—Vlaamse Stovery, *in* Flemish, *and* Les Carbonades Flamades, *in French. Like most classic stews, it has as many versions as there are home cooks who make it. I learned this version when I was working with Ruth Van Waerebeek on our book* Everybody Eats Well in Belgium Cookbook. *Everyone I know who has made this stew keeps it as a repeat recipe.*

Serves 6 to 8

> 4 pounds boneless chuck, cut into 2-inch cubes
> Salt and freshly ground black pepper
> ¹/₄ cup flour, preferably Wondra
> 4 tablespoons unsalted butter
> 3 large onions, cut in half lengthwise and thinly sliced
> 2 12-ounce bottles dark Belgian beer, or other good dark beer
> 2 bay leaves
> 1 tablespoon fresh thyme leaves, or 1 teaspoon dried
> 2 tablespoons red currant jelly or brown sugar
> 1 tablespoon cider vinegar or red vinegar

1. Dry the beef pieces with paper towels. Sprinkle with salt, pepper, and flour. Place 3 tablespoons of the butter in a large, heavy skillet over medium-high heat and when the butter has melted, add the beef cubes in batches so that they do not crowd each other. Brown the cubes evenly on all sides and remove them to a large Dutch oven with a lid.

2. Melt the remaining tablespoon of butter in the skillet over medium-high heat. Add the onions and sauté, stirring frequently with a wooden spoon to scrape up any browned bits from the bottom of the skillet. Sauté until the onions have browned, about 15 minutes, and transfer them to the Dutch oven with the meat.

3. Place the skillet over medium-high heat, add the beer, and stir with a wooden spoon to scrape up any browned bits from the bottom. Bring the beer to a boil and transfer it to the Dutch oven.

4. Add the bay leaves and thyme to the meat and beer mixture and place over very low heat. Cover and simmer for $1\frac{1}{2}$ to 2 hours until the meat is very tender. Stir in the red currant jelly or brown sugar and vinegar just before serving. Taste for seasoning and adjust to taste.

Beef Stew with Red Wine and Shiitake Mushrooms

I first came across a version of this tasty beef stew in March 1996 in Bon Appétit *magazine, and it's been one of my favorites ever since. The shiitake mushrooms add a deep, woodsy flavor, and the baby carrots add sweetness and a pretty look to the stew. Serve with some good crusty bread and a salad on the side.*

Serves 6

3 pounds boneless beef chuck, trimmed of fat and cut into 1^1/$_2$-inch cubes
Salt and freshly ground black pepper
^{1}/$_2$ cup flour, preferably Wondra
4 tablespoons unsalted butter
1 tablespoon olive oil
2 large onions, finely chopped
2 cups dry red wine
1 beef bouillon cube, dissolved in 2 cups hot water
1 tablespoon dark brown sugar
2 cups drained and chopped canned tomatoes
3 tablespoons chopped fresh marjoram, or 1 tablespoon dried
1^1/$_2$ pounds baby Yukon Gold or red-skinned potatoes, peeled and
 quartered
20 baby carrots
1 pound fresh shiitake mushrooms, stems removed, caps sliced into
 ^{3}/$_4$-inch-wide strips

1. Dry the beef pieces with paper towels. Sprinkle with salt, pepper, and flour. Place 2 tablespoons of the butter and the oil in a large heavy skillet over medium-high heat and when the butter has melted, add the beef cubes in batches so that they do not crowd each other. Brown the cubes on one or two sides and remove them to a large Dutch oven with a lid.

2. Melt the remaining 2 tablespoons butter in the skillet over medium-high heat. Add the onions and sauté, stirring frequently with a wooden spoon to scrape up any browned bits from the bottom of the skillet. When the onions have wilted, about 10 minutes, add the wine and beef bouillon to the skillet and cook, stirring, for 1 minute. Transfer the onion mixture to the Dutch oven.

3. Add the sugar, canned tomatoes, and marjoram and stir well. Bring to a boil, reduce heat to medium-low, and simmer, partially covered, for 1½ hours.

4. Uncover the stew, add the potatoes and carrots, and simmer until the potatoes are tender, about 30 minutes. Add the mushrooms and simmer for another 5 minutes, until the mushrooms are tender. Remove from the heat and serve.

Hungarian Gulyás

The original gulyás *(goulash), which goes back to the ninth century, was more of a soup than a stew, but since I love soupy stews, and this simple recipe is so delicious, I decided to include it here. The original version of this recipe appears in* The Cuisine of Hungary, *by George Lang. Serve it with good rye bread and butter.*

Serves 6

3 pounds beef chuck, cut into 1-inch pieces

2 tablespoons canola or vegetable oil

2 large onions, coarsely chopped

2 garlic cloves

Pinch of caraway seeds

Salt

2 tablespoons imported Hungarian sweet paprika

6 cups hot water

1 medium fresh or canned ripe tomato, peeled, seeded, and cut into $1/2$-inch pieces

2 green frying peppers, cored, seeded, and thinly sliced crosswise

1 pound potatoes, peeled and diced

1. Dry the beef cubes with paper towels. Place the oil in a large Dutch oven over medium heat and add the onions. Sauté for 5 minutes until the onions wilt and add the beef cubes. Raise the heat to medium-high and sauté, stirring, until the meat is no longer pink. Remove the pot from the heat.

2. In a mortar and pestle mash the garlic cloves together with the caraway seeds and 1 teaspoon salt.
3. Stir the garlic mixture and paprika into the stew with a wooden spoon and keep stirring until the paprika is absorbed. Pour in the hot water and stir.
4. Place the pot over low heat, cover, and simmer for 1 hour. Add the tomato and green peppers and simmer gently for 30 minutes. Add the potatoes and continue to simmer until the potatoes are cooked through, 20 to 30 minutes.

Short Ribs with Horseradish Sauce

I love to read and cook from W. Park Kerr's books because his recipes are always spicy with chilies and other hot condiments. The inspiration for this recipe comes from his The El Paso Chile Company's Sizzlin' Suppers. *Short ribs, cut into bite-size pieces, replace regular stew meat in this recipe. The bones add extra flavor and texture to this dish. The addition of horseradish sauce at the end lifts the recipe to breathtaking heights. Serve with mashed or baked potatoes and a green vegetable.*

Serves 4 to 6

6 to 8 meaty short ribs (about 4½ to 5 pounds), sawed crosswise in half by
   the butcher
2 tablespoons olive oil
Salt and freshly ground black pepper
2 large onions, cut in half lengthwise and thinly sliced
3 medium carrots, sliced into ½-inch rounds
3 medium celery ribs, thinly sliced
6 garlic cloves, finely chopped
¼ cup all-purpose flour
1 beef bouillon cube, dissolved in 2 cups of hot water
1 cup beer
1 tablespoon tomato paste
1 tablespoon fresh thyme leaves, or 1 teaspoon dried
1 teaspoon caraway seeds

1 bay leaf
2 to 3 tablespoons prepared horseradish

1. Preheat the oven to 325° F.
2. Place the oil in a large heavy skillet over medium-high heat and when the oil starts to shimmer, add the short ribs in batches so that they do not crowd each other. Brown the ribs on all sides and transfer to a large Dutch oven with a lid. Season the ribs with salt and pepper.
3. Add the onions, carrots, celery, and garlic to the skillet and cook, stirring occasionally, until the onion has turned a golden brown, about 12 minutes. Sprinkle with the flour and stir well. Add the bouillon, beer, tomato paste, thyme, caraway, and bay leaf. Stir well and transfer to the Dutch oven with the short ribs.
4. Bring to a simmer over medium-high heat, cover the pot, and place in the oven. Bake for about 2½ hours, until the short ribs are tender. Transfer the ribs to a deep serving bowl. Let the sauce stand for about 5 minutes off the heat. Skim off as much fat as possible from the sauce. Discard the bay leaf. Stir in the horseradish, pour the sauce and vegetables over the short ribs, and serve immediately.

Beef Chili

This is a classic beef chili without the tomatoes, other vegetables, or beans that have been added to the original "bowl of red." If you have never tried chili this way I think you will be amazed at the great, rich flavor of this very American stew. Serve with rice and pinto beans on the side.

Serves 6

>   2 tablespoons olive oil
>   3 pounds lean chuck, cut into ¹/₂-inch pieces
>   6 garlic cloves, finely minced or pushed through a garlic press
>   4 tablespoons mild New Mexico chili powder
>   1 large Knorr beef bouillon cube, dissolved in 4 cups hot water
>   1 tablespoon ground cumin
>   1 tablespoon Mexican oregano, finely crumbled between your fingers
>   2 tablespoons *masa harina* or cornmeal (optional)

1. Place the olive oil in a large Dutch oven over medium-high heat until it is hot but not smoking. Add the beef and sauté, stirring, over high heat until the meat loses its pink color.
2. Turn the heat to very low, add the garlic, and cook, stirring, for 1 minute. Add the chili powder and stir well so the meat is evenly coated. Cook, stirring, for 10 minutes. Slowly add 1 cup of the beef bouillon and mix well.
3. Add the remaining beef bouillon, cumin, and oregano. Simmer, partially covered, over low heat, for 2¹/₂ to 3 hours, until the meat

is very tender, stirring from time to time and adding more water if necessary. About 30 minutes before the chili is done, stir in the *masa harina* or cornmeal if you want to thicken the chili. Then finish simmering for 30 minutes.

Variation

You can use whole dried chilies in place of the chili powder for an even richer chili flavor. Rinse 6 ancho chilies and 4 dried New Mexico chilies. Remove the stems and seeds. Simmer the chilies in 4 cups of water for 30 minutes. Drain the chilies but reserve the cooking water. Place the chilies with 1 cup of the cooking water in a blender or food processor and process to a smooth paste. Add to the beef in step 2, instead of the beef bouillon, and proceed with the rest of the recipe.

Japanese Beef Stew

This is not your usual stew, because the liquids called for are dashi stock and sake. But don't be put off, for it is not hard to make, nor are the ingredients hard to find. If you don't have an Asian store in your neighborhood, go to a health food store, where you can usually find both the kombu *and the bonito flakes.*

Serves 4

FOR DASHI STOCK:

6 cups cold water

1 ounce *kombu* (dried kelp), about 20 square inches

1 cup dried bonito flakes

FOR THE BEEF STEW:

2 pounds boneless beef chuck, cut into 1$^{1}/_{2}$-inch pieces

2 tablespoons canola or peanut oil

1 cup dashi stock

$^{1}/_{2}$ cup sake

1 bunch of scallions, white parts cut off and trimmed, green parts thinly
   sliced

1 pound small red-skinned potatoes, peeled and cut in half

20 baby carrots

3 tablespoons sugar

3 tablespoons light soy sauce

1. Prepare the dashi stock. Place the water and *kombu* in a large
   saucepan over high heat, bring to a boil, and remove from heat.

Let stand for 15 minutes. Remove *kombu* from the water and discard.

2. Sprinkle the bonito flakes into the saucepan and bring to a boil, stirring occasionally. Remove from the heat and let stand for 10 minutes. Pour through a fine sieve or a coffee filter and discard the bonito flakes. Reserve 1 cup of stock and refrigerate or freeze the rest to use for future stews or for making miso soup.

3. Prepare the beef. Pat the beef pieces dry on paper towels. Put the oil in a deep-sided skillet and place over medium-high heat. When the oil is shimmering, add the beef and brown it on all sides. Add 1 cup of dashi stock, the sake, and the white scallion parts. Reduce heat to medium-low and simmer the stew, partially covered, for about 1 hour. Add the potatoes and carrots and enough water to just cover the beef and the vegetables, and simmer for another 25 to 30 minutes, until the beef and the vegetables are tender.

4. When the beef is tender, add the sugar, and simmer, covered, over low heat for 15 minutes. Stir in the soy sauce and sprinkle with the scallion greens.

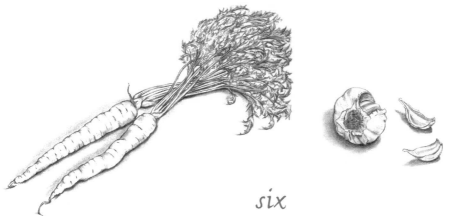

six

___

Lamb Stews

Blanquette d'Agneau

*In many recipes I have come across for Blanquette d'Agneau, the lamb
is blanched before the cooking begins. I prefer Patricia Wells's recipe
from* Bistro Cooking, *because it is so simple to prepare and delicious.
Here is my version, which I like to serve with peeled and boiled new
potatoes and a green salad.*

Serves 6

2 tablespoons unsalted butter

2 tablespoons peanut or canola oil

2$^{1}/_{2}$ pounds boneless lamb from leg or shoulder, cut into 2-inch cubes,
    fat removed

Salt and freshly ground black pepper

6 garlic cloves, peeled and crushed

2 tablespoons flour, preferably Wondra

1 bottle dry white wine, such as sauvignon blanc

2 bay leaves

1 tablespoon fresh thyme leaves, or 1 teaspoon dried

2 large egg yolks

1 tablespoon freshly squeezed lemon juice

2 tablespoons crème fraîche or heavy cream

$^{1}/_{4}$ cup finely chopped fresh chervil or parsley

1. If you have a 12-inch deep-sided heavy skillet or sauté pan with a
   lid, use that for the entire cooking. Otherwise use a heavy skillet
   and a Dutch oven. Put the butter and oil into the skillet over
   medium-high heat. Dry the lamb with paper towels. When the

butter has melted, add enough lamb pieces to make one uncrowded layer. Brown the meat on one or two sides and remove to a platter or Dutch oven. Continue browning the lamb until all the pieces are done.

2. Return all the lamb pieces and their juices to the deep-sided skillet or Dutch oven. Season with salt and pepper. Add the garlic cloves and cook over medium-high heat for 2 to 3 minutes, until you can smell the garlic cooking. Stir well and sprinkle with flour, stirring constantly.

3. Pour in 1 cup of the wine and add the bay leaves and thyme. Simmer the stew for about 5 minutes and add 1 more cup of wine. Cover and simmer over medium-low heat for 1 hour. Add the remaining wine, cover, and simmer for another 30 minutes, or until the meat is tender.

4. In the meantime, whisk together the egg yolks, lemon juice, and cream.

5. When the stew is done, remove the lamb pieces to a warm serving bowl. Turn off the heat under the skillet and whisk the egg yolk mixture into the sauce. Turn the heat back to very low and cook, stirring, until the sauce is smooth and slightly thickened, about 5 minutes. Do not let it come to a boil or it will curdle. Pour the sauce over the meat and serve immediately.

Basque Lamb Stew

One of the best books for meat lovers is Bruce Aidell and Denis Kelly's The Complete Meat Cookbook. *The following, easy-to-prepare lamb stew is based on one of their recipes, in which the lamb is seasoned with a dry, spicy herb rub for a couple of hours before it is cooked. I like the results so much that I often prepare a similar seasoning with other lamb or beef stews.*

Serves 6

2 teaspoons salt
1 tablespoon sweet Hungarian paprika
1 teaspoon chili powder
1 teaspoon dried thyme
$^1/_2$ teaspoon freshly ground black pepper
3 pounds boneless lamb from leg or shoulder, cut into 2-inch cubes,
    fat removed
2 canned or bottled red peppers or pimientos
2 tablespoons red wine vinegar
2 tablespoons olive oil
2 large onions, finely chopped
6 garlic cloves, finely chopped
2 4-ounce cans chopped green chilies
2 bay leaves
1 beef bouillon cube, dissolved in 2 cups hot water
1 cup red wine
Salt and freshly ground black pepper

1. Combine the salt, paprika, chili powder, thyme, and black pepper in a large bowl and mix well. Dry the lamb with paper towels and add the lamb cubes to the spice mixture, mixing well to make sure every piece is covered. Cover and let stand for 2 hours at room temperature. (You can refrigerate the lamb overnight, but remove from the refrigerator 1 hour before cooking.)

2. Place the red peppers and red wine vinegar in a blender or food processor and puree. Set the mixture aside.

3. If you have a 12-inch deep-sided heavy skillet or sauté pan with a lid, use that for the entire cooking. Otherwise use a heavy skillet and a Dutch oven. Put the olive oil into the skillet over medium-high heat. When the oil shimmers, add enough lamb pieces to make one uncrowded layer. Brown the meat on one or two sides and remove to a platter or Dutch oven. Continue browning the lamb until all the pieces are done.

4. Pour off all but 1 tablespoon of oil from the skillet and add the onions, garlic, and green chilies. Sauté over medium heat, stirring frequently with a wooden spoon to scrape up any browned bits on the bottom, until the onions begin to wilt, about 10 minutes. Transfer to the Dutch oven or return all the meat to the deep-sided skillet. Add the pureed red peppers, bay leaves, beef bouillon, and red wine. The liquid should barely cover the lamb. Add more red wine if necessary. Bring to a simmer and cook, partially covered, over medium-low heat for 1½ hours, or until the meat is tender.

5. Remove the meat with a slotted spoon and set aside. Remove and discard the bay leaves. Skim away as much fat as possible from the broth, or pour it through a degreaser. Return to the skillet and boil over high heat for about 10 minutes to reduce the sauce. Return the meat to the sauce and simmer over medium heat for 5 minutes to reheat the meat, and serve.

Lamb Stew with Spring Vegetables

Back in the early sixties when I was learning to cook from Simone Beck, Louisette Bertholle, and Julia Child's revolutionary book Mastering the Art of French Cooking, *this French lamb stew,* Navarin Printanier, *was the first really good stew I ever made, and to this day it remains one of the best stews in my repertoire. Here is my latest version.*

Serves 6

3 pounds boneless lamb from leg or shoulder, cut into 2-inch cubes,
   fat removed

3 tablespoons flour, preferably Wondra

1 tablespoon sugar

1 teaspoon salt

$1/2$ teaspoon freshly ground black pepper

1 tablespoon unsalted butter

2 tablespoons olive oil

3 medium yellow onions, finely chopped

6 garlic cloves, finely chopped

1 beef bouillon cube, dissolved in 3 cups hot water

1 cup drained and chopped canned tomatoes

1 teaspoon fresh thyme leaves, or $1/2$ teaspoon dried

1 teaspoon finely chopped fresh rosemary leaves

1 bay leaf

12 small new potatoes, peeled and quartered

6 carrots, peeled and cut into 1-inch lengths
3 parsnips, peeled, cut in half lengthwise, and cut into 1-inch lengths
1 10-ounce package frozen small white onions, thawed
1^1/$_2$ cups fresh shelled peas or 2 cups frozen peas, thawed
1^1/$_2$ cups fresh peeled asparagus, cut into 1-inch pieces

1. Preheat the oven to 350° F.
2. Dry the lamb with paper towels. Combine flour, sugar, salt, and pepper in a small bowl and mix well. Sprinkle the lamb pieces with the flour mixture. Place the butter and 1 tablespoon of the olive oil in a large heavy skillet over medium-high heat and when the butter has melted, add the lamb cubes in batches so that they do not crowd each other. Brown the cubes on one or two sides and remove them to a large Dutch oven with a lid.
3. Add the remaining olive oil, the onions, and the garlic to the skillet and sauté over medium-high heat, stirring frequently with a wooden spoon to scrape up any browned bits from the bottom of the skillet. When the onions have wilted, about 10 minutes, add the bouillon to the skillet and cook, stirring, for 1 minute.
4. Transfer the contents of the skillet to the Dutch oven. Bring to a simmer over medium heat and cook for 2 minutes, stirring frequently. Add the tomatoes, thyme, rosemary, and bay leaf. There should be enough liquid to almost cover the meat. If necessary, add a little more water, or a splash of red or white wine. Return to a simmer, cover the Dutch oven, and place it in

the oven. Check the stew in 15 minutes and reduce the heat if necessary, so that the stew simmers gently for another 45 minutes.

5. Add the potatoes, carrots, parsnips, and onions. Stir well, bring to a simmer on top of the stove, and return to the oven for 30 minutes. Remove from the oven and season to taste with salt and pepper. Add the peas and asparagus and return to the oven for another 20 to 30 minutes, until the green vegetables are tender. Remove from the oven and serve.

Lamb Stew with Dill Sauce

This simple and easy-to-make lamb stew derives originally from Scandinavia, where dill is a major herb, sometimes used in such large quantities that it is almost a vegetable. This recipe is no exception. Serve over mashed or boiled potatoes.

Serves 6

> 3 pounds boneless lamb from leg or shoulder, cut into 2-inch cubes,
>   fat removed
> 3 cups chicken broth
> 2 cups water
> 2 leeks, white parts with 1 inch of pale green
> 1 large carrot, peeled and cut into 3 pieces
> 1 large bunch of fresh dill with stems, tied into a bouquet with kitchen
>   string
> 8 white peppercorns
> 1 teaspoon salt
> 2 tablespoons unsalted butter
> 2 tablespoons all-purpose flour
> 1 tablespoon white wine vinegar
> 2 teaspoons sugar
> ¼ cup chopped fresh dill
> 2 tablespoons heavy cream

1. Place the lamb, chicken broth, water, leeks, carrot, dill, peppercorns, and salt into a large heavy pot. Bring to a boil over medium-high heat and skim away any foam that rises to the

surface. Reduce heat to low and simmer for 1½ hours, or until the meat is tender.

2. Remove stew from the heat and strain the broth into a medium saucepan. Place the broth over medium-high heat and boil until it reduces almost by half, 6 to 8 minutes. Remove from heat. In the meantime, remove the lamb cubes from the vegetables and discard the vegetables.

3. Melt the butter in a medium saucepan over medium-low heat. Whisk in the flour and continue whisking for 1 minute. Gradually whisk in the reduced broth and continue cooking over medium heat, whisking from time to time, until the sauce thickens, about 5 minutes. Whisk in the white vinegar, sugar, fresh chopped dill, and heavy cream. Simmer for a few minutes to blend the flavors, then add the lamb and simmer for 2 to 3 more minutes, to heat the lamb through. Season to taste with salt and pepper and serve.

Irish Lamb Stew with Stout

Many Irish stew recipes call for water as the required liquid. But ever since I tasted a recipe very similar to this one, made with flavorful Irish stout, I have never gone back. If you can't find Irish stout, substitute a good dark ale or beer.

Serves 6

2¹/₂ pounds boneless lamb from leg or shoulder, cut into 1¹/₂-inch cubes,
    fat removed
2 tablespoons butter
2 tablespoons peanut or canola oil
Salt and freshly ground black pepper
3 large leeks, white part plus 1 inch of green, thinly sliced
2 medium-size onions, coarsely chopped
1 6-ounce bottle Irish stout or other dark ale or beer
4 carrots, peeled and cut into 1-inch pieces
2 parsnips, peeled and cut into 1-inch pieces
2 large potatoes (1¹/₂ to 2 pounds), peeled and cubed
1 tablespoon fresh thyme leaves, or 1 teaspoon dried
1 beef bouillon cube, dissolved in 2 cups hot water
2 slices whole-grain bread
2 tablespoons grainy Dijon mustard
¹/₂ cup finely chopped flat-leaf parsley

1. Preheat the oven to 350° F.
2. Dry the lamb with paper towels. Place the butter and oil in a large heavy skillet over medium-high heat and when the butter has

melted, add the lamb cubes in batches so that they do not crowd each other. Brown the cubes on one or two sides and remove them to a large Dutch oven with a lid. Sprinkle with salt and pepper.

3. Add the leeks and onions to the skillet and sauté over medium-high heat, stirring frequently with a wooden spoon to scrape up any browned bits from the bottom of the skillet. When the onions have wilted, about 10 minutes, add the stout to the skillet and cook, stirring, for 1 minute.

4. Transfer the contents of the skillet to the Dutch oven. Add the carrots, parsnips, potatoes, and thyme. Pour in the beef bouillon. Spread the bread slices on one side with mustard and place them, mustard side down, over the stew. Cover with the lid and place in preheated oven. Cook for 1½ hours, or until the meat is tender.

5. Remove from oven, uncover, and stir well to mix in the bread. Season to taste with salt and pepper. Sprinkle with parsley and serve.

Variations

1. This stew also works well with beef.
2. Instead of using butter, chop 4 thick slices of bacon and cook them until all the fat is rendered and the bacon pieces are crisp. Remove the bacon pieces and use the bacon fat for browning the meat and sautéing the vegetables. When the stew is done, sprinkle the top with the bacon pieces along with the chopped parsley.

Lamb Stew with Chickpeas, Apricots, and Raisins

Here is a lamb stew enriched with chickpeas and made sweet and savory with apricots, raisins, and spices. Serve it over basmati rice for a lovely, special dinner.

Serves 6

$1/2$ teaspoon salt

$1/2$ teaspoon ground cardamom

$1/2$ teaspoon ground cinnamon

$1/2$ teaspoon freshly ground black pepper

$1/4$ to $1/2$ teaspoon cayenne pepper

$2^1/2$ pounds boneless lamb from leg or shoulder, cut into 2-inch cubes, fat removed

2 tablespoons peanut or canola oil

3 large onions, finely chopped

6 large shallots, finely chopped

6 garlic cloves, finely chopped

1 tablespoon finely chopped fresh ginger

2 cups water

2 to 3 cups canned drained chickpeas

$3/4$ cup quartered dried apricots

$1/4$ cup golden raisins

1 tablespoon fresh lemon juice or white wine vinegar

1 teaspoon sugar (optional)

1. Place the salt, cardamom, cinnamon, black pepper, and cayenne in a large bowl and mix well. Dry the lamb with paper towels, add the lamb cubes, and toss well so that every piece is coated.

2. Place the oil in a large heavy skillet over medium-high heat. When the oil shimmers, add enough lamb pieces to make a single uncrowded layer. Brown the meat on one or two sides and remove to a Dutch oven. Continue browning the lamb until all the pieces are done.

3. Add the onions, shallots, garlic, and ginger to the skillet and sauté, stirring frequently with a wooden spoon to scrape up any browned bits from the bottom. When the onions have wilted, about 10 minutes, remove them to the Dutch oven. Pour the water into skillet and cook, stirring, for a few minutes, then add the water to the Dutch oven. Add the chickpeas, stir well, and place over medium-high heat. Bring the stew to a boil, reduce the heat to medium-low, and simmer, covered, for 1 hour.

4. Remove the lid, add the apricots and raisins, and simmer, uncovered, for another 20 to 30 minutes, until the meat is very tender and the sauce is reduced and slightly thickened. Stir in the lemon juice and sugar, if using, and serve.

Lamb Stew with Chilies and Cilantro

This is a satisfying spicy stew with great flavors. It is almost like a chili, but uses fresh green jalapeños to provide the heat rather than dried red chili pepper. The cilantro and cumin really liven it up. Serve the stew with rice or mashed potatoes.

Serves 6

2¹/₂ pounds boneless lamb from leg or shoulder, cut into 2-inch cubes, fat removed

Salt and freshly ground black pepper

2 tablespoons olive oil

2 large onions, coarsely chopped

6 garlic cloves, finely chopped

4 jalapeño chilies, seeded and finely chopped

1 tablespoon ground cumin

1 cup dry red wine

¹/₂ beef bouillon cube, dissolved in 1 cup hot water

3 cups drained and chopped canned tomatoes

¹/₂ cup finely chopped fresh cilantro stems

¹/₂ cup chopped fresh cilantro leaves

1. Dry the lamb cubes on paper towels and sprinkle them with salt and pepper. If you have a 12-inch deep-sided heavy skillet or sauté pan with a lid, use that for the entire cooking. Otherwise use a heavy skillet and a Dutch oven. Put the olive oil into the

skillet over medium-high heat. When the oil shimmers, add enough lamb pieces to make one uncrowded layer. Brown the meat on one or two sides and remove to a platter or Dutch oven. Continue browning the lamb until all the pieces are done.

2. Add the onions, garlic, jalapeños, and cumin to the skillet. Sauté over medium heat, stirring frequently with a wooden spoon to scrape up any browned bits on the bottom, until the onions begin to wilt, about 10 minutes. Add the red wine and cook, stirring, for another 3 minutes, then transfer to the Dutch oven if that is what you are using.

3. Add the bouillon, tomatoes, and chopped cilantro stems. Stir and bring the stew to a boil over medium-high heat. Reduce heat to medium-low and simmer, covered, for 1¹/₂ hours, or until the meat is tender. Season with salt and pepper to taste, sprinkle with chopped cilantro leaves, and serve.

Lamb, Sausage, and White Bean Stew

This recipe is based on the idea of a cassoulet, but one that is much simpler to make and uses a lot less fat. Serve it with good, crispy bread and a green salad.

Serves 6

$2^1/2$ pounds boneless lamb from leg or shoulder, cut into $1^1/2$-inch cubes, fat removed

Salt and freshly ground black pepper

$1/4$ cup flour, preferably Wondra

1 tablespoon unsalted butter

1 tablespoon olive oil

3 medium onions, cut in half and thinly sliced

6 garlic cloves, finely chopped

4 carrots, peeled and cut into 2-inch chunks

1 pound andouille or kielbasa sausage

1 cup dry red wine

1 beef bouillon cube, dissolved in 2 cups hot water

2 cups drained and chopped canned tomatoes

1 teaspoon fresh thyme leaves, or $1/2$ teaspoon dried

1 bay leaf

2 19-ounce cans cannellini or Great Northern beans, drained and rinsed

$1/2$ cup homemade bread crumbs

3 tablespoons unsalted butter, melted

1. Dry the lamb cubes on paper towels, sprinkle them with salt and pepper, and dust them with flour. Place the butter and oil in a large heavy skillet over medium-high heat and when the butter has melted, add the lamb cubes in batches so that they do not crowd each other. Brown the cubes on one or two sides and remove them to a large Dutch oven with a lid.

2. Add the onions, garlic, carrots, and sausage to the skillet and sauté over medium-high heat, stirring frequently with a wooden spoon to scrape up any browned bits from the bottom of the skillet. When the onions have wilted, about 10 minutes, add the wine to the skillet and cook, stirring, for 1 minute. Transfer everything to the Dutch oven.

3. Place the Dutch oven over medium-high heat and add the bouillon, tomatoes, thyme, and bay leaf and bring to a boil, stirring occasionally. Reduce the heat to medium-low and simmer, partially covered, for 1 hour.

4. In the meantime, preheat the oven to 350° F.

5. Stir in the beans, sprinkle bread crumbs over the top, and drizzle melted butter over the bread crumbs. Place, uncovered, in the oven and bake for 1 hour until the meat is very tender. Remove from the oven and serve.

Pork Stews

Sweet and Savory Pork Stew with Fruit

A spicy pork stew sweetened with the rich flavors of dried fruit makes a perfect winter meal on a cold night.

Serves 6

3 pounds lean boneless pork, cut into 2-inch cubes
Salt and freshly ground black pepper
2 tablespoons unsalted butter
2 tablespoons peanut or canola oil
2 large onions, cut in half and sliced
6 garlic cloves, finely chopped
2 tablespoons all-purpose flour
1 1/2 cups apple cider or juice
1 cup dark beer or ale
2 tablespoons Dijon mustard
1 teaspoon ground coriander
1/4 teaspoon ground cinnamon
1/4 teaspoon cayenne pepper
1 cup chopped dried apricots
1 cup chopped pitted prunes

1. Preheat the oven to 350° F.
2. Dry the pork cubes on paper towels. Sprinkle with salt and pepper. Place 1 tablespoon of the butter and 1 tablespoon of the oil in a large heavy skillet over medium-high heat and when the

butter has melted, add the pork cubes in batches so that they do not crowd each other. Brown the cubes on one or two sides and remove them to a large enameled Dutch oven with a lid.

3. Add the remaining butter and oil and the onions and garlic to the skillet and sauté over medium-high heat, stirring frequently with a wooden spoon to scrape up any browned bits from the bottom of the skillet. When the onions have wilted, about 10 minutes, add the flour and stir for 3 minutes. Mix the cider, beer, or ale and mustard together, add to the skillet, and cook, stirring, for 1 minute. Pour the broth and onions into the Dutch oven, then stir in the coriander, cinnamon, and cayenne. Finally stir in the apricots and prunes.

4. Cover the Dutch oven and place it into the preheated oven for 1 hour. Remove the lid from the Dutch oven and bake another 20 to 30 minutes, until the pork is very tender and the broth has a saucy consistency.

Sausage and Tomato Stew

Here is a quick and easy stew rich with the flavor of sausages, tomatoes, and peppers. Serve the stew with mashed potatoes or over buttered noodles.

Serves 6

$1/4$ cup olive oil
$1^{1}/_{2}$ pounds sweet Italian sausage, cut into $^{1}/_{2}$-inch slices
$1^{1}/_{2}$ pounds hot Italian sausage, cut into $^{1}/_{2}$-inch slices
2 large onions, cut lengthwise and sliced
6 garlic cloves, finely minced or pushed through a garlic press
2 yellow bell peppers, cored, seeded, and chopped
2 red bell peppers, cored, seeded, and chopped
1 28-ounce can tomatoes, drained and roughly chopped
1 cup dry red wine
$^{1}/_{2}$ cup finely chopped fresh Italian parsley
Salt and freshly ground black pepper

1. Place 2 tablespoons of the olive oil in a large skillet over medium-high heat. Add the sliced sausage and cook, stirring frequently, until the sausage is well browned.
2. Add the onions and garlic and cook over medium heat for another 5 minutes, until the onions start to wilt. Transfer the sausage and onions to a large Dutch oven.
3. Add the remaining 2 tablespoons olive oil to the skillet and sauté the peppers over medium-high heat for 7 to 8 minutes, until they

start to wilt. Transfer the peppers to the Dutch oven and mix well with the sausages and onions.

4. Place the Dutch oven over medium heat and stir in the tomatoes, wine, and parsley. Simmer, uncovered, for 30 minutes. Taste for seasoning and add salt and freshly ground black pepper to taste.

Pork Stew with Cider, Carrots, and Lima Beans

Prepare this lovely autumn stew when fresh apple cider is available. The combination of the tart-sweet cider and the delicate, lean pork is a happy one, and the carrots and lima beans add to the tastiness of the stew. The stew has the advantage of being extremely low in fat and calories.

Serves 6

> **3 pounds pork tenderloin, cut into 1-inch cubes**
> **Salt and freshly ground black pepper**
> **$1/3$ cup all-purpose flour**
> **3 tablespoons olive oil**
> **2 large onions, cut in half lengthwise and thinly sliced**
> **3 cups fresh apple cider**
> **$1^1/2$ cups chicken broth**
> **1 pound baby carrots**
> **1 10-ounce package frozen baby lima beans, thawed**

1. Dry the pork cubes on paper towels. Sprinkle with salt, pepper, and flour. Place 2 tablespoons of the olive oil in a large heavy skillet over medium-high heat and when the oil starts to shimmer, add the pork cubes in batches so that they do not crowd each other. Brown the cubes on one or two sides and remove them to a large enameled Dutch oven with a lid.

2. Add the remaining olive oil to the skillet and place over medium heat. Add the onions and sauté, stirring, for 5 minutes until they start to wilt. Gradually add the cider and chicken broth, stirring with a wooden spoon to scrape up any browned bits from the bottom of the skillet.

3. Transfer the onions and liquid to the Dutch oven. Place over medium heat and bring to a simmer. Reduce heat to low, cover, and simmer for 1 hour. Remove the lid, add the carrots and baby lima beans, and simmer for 20 to 30 minutes, until the meat is very tender and the carrots and lima beans are cooked through.

Pork Stew with Red Wine and Paprika

A rich and flavorful stew, this is based on a recipe from Mario Batali, one of the best Italian chefs in New York. I like to serve the stew with mashed potatoes or buttered noodles, with a salad on the side.

Serves 4

> 2 pounds lean boneless pork, cut into 2-inch cubes
> Salt and freshly ground black pepper
> $1/4$ cup olive oil
> 2 large onions, cut lengthwise and sliced
> 1 tablespoon Hungarian hot paprika
> 2 cups drained and chopped canned tomatoes
> 1 cup dry red wine
> 2 cups chicken broth
> 2 bay leaves
> 1 tablespoon fresh marjoram leaves, or 1 teaspoon dried
> 1 sprig fresh rosemary
> 2 tablespoons freshly squeezed lemon juice

1. Dry the pork cubes on paper towels and sprinkle with salt and pepper. Place 2 tablespoons of the olive oil in a large heavy skillet over medium-high heat and when the oil starts to shimmer, add the pork cubes in batches so that they do not crowd each other. Brown the cubes on one or two sides and remove them to a large enameled Dutch oven with a lid.

2. Add the remaining olive oil to the skillet and place over medium heat. Add the onions and sauté, stirring, for 10 minutes until they are soft and start to brown. Add the paprika and cook, stirring, for 5 minutes. Add the tomatoes and red wine. Cook, stirring with a wooden spoon to scrape up any browned bits from the bottom, until the wine has mostly cooked away. Transfer the onion and wine mixture to the Dutch oven.

3. Add the chicken broth, bay leaves, marjoram, and rosemary. Bring to a boil, reduce heat to low, cover, and simmer for $1\frac{1}{2}$ hours, until the meat is tender. Remove the bay leaves and rosemary sprig. Stir in the lemon juice, season to taste with salt and pepper, and serve.

Pork Green Chili Stew

This green chili stew is popular throughout the Southwest United States, with some regional variations. A more authentic New Mexican version would omit the tomatoes and potatoes, for a rather stark but equally delicious stew. Serve over rice, or with tortillas.

Serves 6

3 pounds lean boneless pork, cut into 2-inch cubes
Salt and freshly ground black pepper
3 tablespoons olive oil
2 large onions, finely chopped
6 garlic cloves, finely chopped
1 cup dry white wine
3 4-ounce cans chopped green chilies
2 fresh jalapeño chilies, halved, seeded, and thinly sliced
2 cups drained and chopped canned tomatoes
1 beef bouillon cube, dissolved in 3 cups boiling water
$^1/_2$ cup finely chopped fresh cilantro stems
$^1/_2$ teaspoon oregano
2 to 3 large potatoes peeled and cut into $^1/_2$-inch cubes
$^1/_2$ cup chopped fresh cilantro leaves
Tabasco or other hot pepper sauce
Lime wedges

1. Dry the pork cubes on paper towels. Sprinkle with salt and pepper. Place 2 tablespoons of the olive oil in a large heavy skillet over medium-high heat and when the oil starts to shimmer, add

127

the pork cubes in batches so that they do not crowd each other. Brown the cubes on one or two sides and remove them to a large enameled Dutch oven with a lid.

2. Add the remaining 1 tablespoon of olive oil with the onions and garlic to the skillet and sauté over medium-high heat, stirring frequently with a wooden spoon to scrape up any browned bits from the bottom of the skillet. When the onions have wilted, about 10 minutes, add the wine to the skillet and cook, stirring, for 1 minute. Pour the wine and onions into the Dutch oven and stir to mix with the pork cubes. Then add the canned green chilies, jalapeño chilies, tomatoes, bouillon, cilantro stems, and oregano. Stir well.

3. Place the Dutch oven over medium-high heat and bring to a simmer. Reduce heat to low, cover, and simmer gently for 1½ hours. Add the diced potatoes and simmer, partially covered, for another 20 to 30 minutes, until the potatoes are cooked through and the meat is very tender. Serve with hot sauce and lime wedges on the side.

Chinese Sparerib Stew

I based this recipe on one I found by the late Barbara Tropp, who specialized in Chinese cooking. If you cannot find Chinese black beans in your market, go to a Chinese restaurant and ask if they will sell you some. Serve the stew over rice with a green vegetable on the side.

Serves 6

¼ cup **Chinese black beans, coarsely chopped**

6 to 8 **large garlic cloves, peeled and lightly smashed**

3 tablespoons **soy sauce**

3 teaspoons **sugar**

1¼ cups **hot water**

3 pounds **meaty pork spareribs, cut crosswise into 1-inch-wide strips of riblets (ask your butcher to do this for you)**

2 tablespoons **peanut or canola oil**

½ to ¾ teaspoon **dried red chili flakes, or to taste**

6 **scallions, trimmed and thinly sliced into rings, half of the green part and all of the white part**

1. Combine the black beans, garlic, soy sauce, sugar, and water in a bowl. Stir to dissolve the sugar and set aside.
2. Trim fat away from the ribs. Cut the strips of ribs between the bones into individual pieces.
3. Choose a deep-sided skillet or sauté pan large enough to hold all the sparerib nuggets. Place over high heat for a minute and add the oil, swirling it to cover the bottom of the pan. Add the

sparerib nuggets and sauté them, stirring and tossing, for about 5 minutes, until all the meat has turned gray.

4. Add the chili flakes and stir. Then add the sauce, mix well, and bring the mixture to a boil. Reduce the heat to low, cover the pan, and cook for about 45 minutes, stirring occasionally, until the meat is tender enough to pull away from the bone.

5. Drain the ribs over a bowl. Use a fat separator to remove the excess fat from the sauce, or refrigerate until the fat solidifies and can be removed. Return the rib nuggets to the sauce and reheat slowly over low heat, but do not boil.

6. Place a mound of rice, if using, in each bowl, and top with sparerib stew. Garnish with scallions and serve.

Pork and Yam Stew with Mustard

The sweet flavor of the yams and the spiciness of the mustard make a great backdrop for the flavorful pork cubes. Serve this stew with crusty bread and a green salad with sliced apples in it.

Serves 6

> 3 pounds lean boneless pork, cut into 2-inch cubes
> Salt and freshly ground black pepper
> $1/3$ cup flour, preferably Wondra
> 3 tablespoons olive oil
> 2 medium onions, finely chopped
> 6 garlic cloves, finely chopped
> 1 cup chicken broth
> 1 cup dry sherry
> $1/4$ cup Dijon mustard
> 2 tablespoons brown sugar
> 2 medium yams, cut into 1-inch cubes
> $1/3$ cup finely chopped fresh dill
> $1/4$ cup finely chopped fresh parsley

1. Preheat the oven to 350° F.
2. Dry the pork cubes on paper towels. Sprinkle with salt, pepper, and flour. Place 2 tablespoons of the olive oil in a large heavy skillet over medium-high heat and when the oil starts to shimmer, add the pork cubes in batches so that they do not crowd each

other. Brown the cubes on one or two sides and remove them to a large enameled Dutch oven with a lid.

3. Add the remaining 1 tablespoon of olive oil with the onions and garlic to the skillet and sauté over medium-high heat, stirring frequently with a wooden spoon to scrape up any browned bits from the bottom of the skillet. When the onions have wilted, about 10 minutes, add the broth and wine to the skillet and cook, stirring, for 1 minute. Pour the broth and onions into the Dutch oven, then stir in the mustard and brown sugar. Add the yam cubes and stir.

4. Cover the Dutch oven and place it in the preheated oven for 1 to 1½ hours, until the pork and yams are tender.

5. Season with salt and pepper to taste, garnish with dill and parsley, and serve.

Sausage and Clam Stew

This recipe is based on a Portuguese pork stew with clams called Cataplana*, which is also the name of the round, lidded pot in which it is cooked. In this version the pork is replaced with Italian sausage, for a much quicker-cooking stew. The result is irresistible and doesn't require much more than a crusty bread to go with it.*

Serves 6

1 tablespoon olive oil
2$^{1}/_{2}$ pounds Italian sausage
1 large onion, finely chopped
6 garlic cloves, finely chopped
1 teaspoon sweet paprika
1 cup drained and chopped canned tomatoes
$^{1}/_{2}$ cup bottled clam juice
$^{1}/_{2}$ cup dry white wine
2 bay leaves
Large pinch of dried red pepper flakes, or to taste
24 littleneck clams, scrubbed
$^{1}/_{4}$ cup finely chopped flat-leaf parsley
Salt and freshly ground black pepper

1. Heat the olive oil in a large skillet over medium-high heat until it shimmers. Prick the sausages all over with a fork and add them to the heated skillet. Sauté them, turning frequently, until they are browned, about 10 minutes. Remove the sausages to a cutting board and pour out all but 2 tablespoons of the fat from the skillet.

2. Add the onion and about half the chopped garlic and sauté over medium-high heat, stirring frequently with a wooden spoon to scrape up any browned bits from the bottom of the skillet. When the onion has wilted, about 10 minutes, add the paprika and cook, stirring, for 1 minute longer. Transfer the onion mixture to a larger pot off the heat. Slice the sausages into $1/2$-inch pieces and add them to the pot, together with the chopped tomatoes.

3. Put the clam juice, white wine, the remaining chopped garlic, bay leaves, and red pepper flakes in a stainless steel saucepan large enough to hold the clams. Discard any clams that are broken. Add the clams to the saucepan, cover, and bring to a boil. Cook over medium-high heat, shaking the pot occasionally, for about 5 minutes. Open the lid, remove any opened clams to a bowl, cover, and continue to cook, shaking the pot from time to time, for another 5 minutes. Remove the opened clams and cook, covered, any unopened clams that remain. After 5 minutes, remove the opened clams and discard any that have not opened.

4. Pour the clam liquid carefully into the sausage mixture, leaving any grit behind in the bottom of the pan. Add the parsley and season with salt and pepper to taste. Add the clams, with or without their shells, cover, and simmer over low heat until everything warms through.

Index

Aidell, Bruce, 99

Alsatian beef, lamb, and pork stew, 77–78

Alsatian Coq au Riesling, 43

anchovies, veal stew with olives, basil and, 71–72

apple cider
  carrots and lima beans, pork stew with, 123–24
  and parsnips, chicken stew with, 53–54

apples, Moroccan chicken stew with, 55

apricots, chickpeas, raisins and, lamb stew with, 111–12

At Home in Provence (Wells), 81

autumn vegetable stew, 7–8

Baekeoffe (baker's oven), 77

basil, veal stew with olives, anchovies and, 71–72

Basque lamb stew, 99–101

Batali, Mario, 125

bean(s)
  black, chili, 15–16
  black, Chinese, 129
  green, chickpea, potato, and zucchini stew, 13–14
  lima, apple cider and carrots, pork stew with, 123–24
  shrimp in green chili sauce with, 35–36
  and spinach, veal and sausage stew with, 73–74
  white, lamb and sausage stew, 115–16

Beck, Simone, 103

beef
  bulgur as substitute for, 15
  chili, 91–92
  lamb and pork stew, Alsatian, 77–78
  onion stew with, 79–80
  as substitute for lamb, 110

beef stew
  Flemish, with beer, 83–84
  Japanese, 93–94
  with red wine and shiitake mushrooms, 85–86
  with white wine and mustard, 81–82

beer
  Flemish beef stew with, 83–84

beer *(continued)*
    stout, Irish lamb stew with,
        109–10
Bertholle, Louisette, 103
Bistro Cooking (Wells), 51, 97
Bittman, Mark, 49
black bean(s)
    chili, 15–16
    Chinese, 129
Blanquette d'Agneau, 97–98
Blanquette de Veau, 59–61
Boehm, Arthur, 25
Bon Appétit, 85
bonito flakes, 93
bouillabaisse-style chicken stew,
    51–52
Brown, Edward, 25
browning meat, x, xi
bulgur, as substitute for beef, 15

cacciatore, chicken, 45–46
carrots
    apple cider and lima beans, pork
        stew with, 123–24
    parsnips, and potatoes, veal stew
        with, 69–70
cassoulet, 115

Catalan seafood stew, 19–20
Cataplana stew, 133–34
cheese. *See* feta cheese
chicken
    cacciatore, 45–46
    marinating, 51
    paprikash, 47–48
    with Riesling wine, 43–44
    seafood and sausage gumbo,
        37–39
    substituting, for veal, 63
    with wine and prunes, 49–50
chicken stew
    with apple cider and parsnips,
        53–54
    bouillabaisse-style, 51–52
    Moroccan, with apples, 55
chickpeas
    apricots and raisins, lamb stew
        with, 111–12
    green bean, potato, and zucchini
        stew, 13–14
Child, Julia, 103
chili, green
    pork, stew, 127–28
    sauce with beans, shrimp in,
        35–36
Chili! (Robbins), 15

chili(es)
  beef, 91–92
  black bean, 15–16
  chocolate in, 15
  and cilantro, lamb stew with,
    113–14
  jalapeño, 113
  jalapeño sauce with, 36
  variations for, 92
  for vegetarians, 15
Chinese black beans, 129
Chinese sparerib stew, 129–30
chocolate, in chili, 15
cilantro and chilies, lamb stew with,
    113–14
clam, sausage and, stew,
    133–34
clams, unopened, 23
Complete Meat Cookbook, The
    (Aidell/Kelly), 99
Coq au Riesling, Alsatian, 43
Coq au Vin, with prunes, 49
corn
  and shrimp stew, 33–34
  stew, Maquechoux, 33–34
  and tomatoes, monkfish and
    scallop stew with, 27–28
cream, as addition, 59

Creole Gumbo and All That Jazz
    (Mitcham), 37
Cuisine of Hungary, The (Lang), 87
curry, quick shrimp, 29–30

dashi stock, 93
dill sauce, lamb stew with, 107–8
Dutch oven, xi

egg yolks, as addition, 43, 59
*El Paso Chile Company's Sizzlin'
    Suppers, The* (Kerr), 89
*Everybody Eats Well in Belgium
    Cookbook* (Van Waerebeek/
    Robbins), 83

fennel and mustard, veal stew with,
    65–66
feta cheese, 13
  shrimp stew and, 31
  in Stifado, 79
fish. *See also* seafood, sausage, and
    chicken gumbo; seafood stews;
    specific fish; specific seafood
  bouillabaisse, 51

fish (*continued*)
　　substituting seafood and, 21
Flemish beef stew with beer,
　　83–84
freezing stews, ix, xi
fruit, 55
　　dried, 55, 111, 119
　　sweet and savory pork stew with,
　　　119–20

Great Fish, Quick (Revsin),
　　21
Greek stews, 13–14, 79–80
green chili
　　pork, stew, 127–28
　　sauce with beans, shrimp in,
　　　35–36
gulyás, Hungarian, 87–88
gumbo, seafood, sausage and
　　chicken, 37–39

herb rub, 99
horseradish sauce, short ribs with,
　　89–90
Hungarian gulyás, 87–88
Hungarian stew, 47–48

Irish lamb stew with stout,
　　109–10

jalapeño chilies, 113
jalapeño sauce with chili, 36
Japanese beef stew, 93–94

Kelly, Denis, 99
Kerr, W. Park, 89
kombu, 93

lamb
　　beef and pork stew, Alsatian, 77–78
　　beef as substitute for, 110
　　sausage and white bean stew,
　　　115–16
lamb stew, 97–98
　　Basque, 99–101
　　with chickpeas, apricots and
　　　raisins, 111–12
　　with chilies and cilantro, 113–14
　　with dill sauce, 107–8
　　Irish, with stout, 109–10
　　with spring vegetables, 103–5
　　variations for, 110

Lang, George, 87
lentil, potato, and spinach stew,
    11–12
Les Carbonades Flamades, 83–84
Leslie Revsin's seafood stew, 21–23
low fat stew, 123–24

Madison, Deborah, 3
Maquechoux corn stew, 33–34
Marengo, veal stew, 63–64
marinating
    chicken, 51
    meat, 77, 78
Mastering the Art of French Cooking
    (Beck/Bertholle/Child), 103
meat
    browning, x, xi, 59
    marinating, 77, 78
Mitcham, Howard, 37
Modern Seafood Cook, The
    (Brown/Boehm), 25
monkfish
    and scallop stew with corn and
        tomatoes, 27–28
    stewed in red wine, 25–26
Moroccan chicken stew with apples,
    55

mushrooms, shiitake, red wine and,
    beef stew with, 85–86
mustard
    fennel and, veal stew with, 65–66
    pork and yam stew with, 131–32
    white wine and, beef stew with,
        81–82

Napoleon's chef, 63
Navarin Printanier, 103–5
New York Times, 49
nuts. *See* pine nuts; walnuts

olives, anchovies, and basil, veal
    stew with, 71–72
onion
    red, salsa, 16
    stew, with beef, 79–80

paprika and red wine, pork stew
    with, 125–26
paprikash, chicken, 47–48
parsnips
    apple cider and, chicken stew
        with, 53–54

parsnips (*continued*)
  carrots and potatoes, veal stew
    with, 69–70
Pernod, 19
pine nuts, 19
pork
  green chili stew, 127–28
  and yam stew with mustard,
    131–32
pork stew
  Alsatian beef, lamb and,
    77–78
  with apple cider, carrots, and lima
    beans, 123–24
  Portuguese, 133–34
  with red wine and paprika,
    125–26
  sweet and savory, with fruit,
    119–20
Portuguese pork stew, 133–34
potatoes
  carrots and parsnips, veal stew
    with, 69–70
  green bean, chickpea, and
    zucchini stew, 13–14
  lentil and spinach stew, 11–12
prunes
  Coq au Vin with, 49

wine and, chicken with,
  49–50

quick shrimp curry, 29–30

ragout, spring veal, 67–68
raisins, chickpeas and apricots, lamb
  stew with, 111–12
refrigerating stews, x
Revsin, Leslie, 21
  seafood stew, 21–23
ribs. *See* Chinese sparerib stew;
  short ribs with horseradish
  sauce

salsa, red onion, 16
sauce
  dill, lamb stew with, 107–8
  green chili, with beans, shrimp in,
    35–36
  horseradish, short ribs with,
    89–90
  jalapeño, with chili, 36
sausage
  and clam stew, 133–34

lamb and white bean stew,
115–16
seafood, and chicken gumbo,
37–39
and tomato stew, 121–22
sausage stew, veal and, with beans
and spinach, 73–74
scallop and monkfish stew with corn
and tomatoes, 27–28
seafood, sausage, and chicken
gumbo, 37–39
seafood stews
Catalan, 19–20
Leslie Revsin's, 21–23
shiitake mushrooms and red wine,
beef stew with, 85–86
short ribs with horseradish sauce,
89–90
shrimp
and corn stew, 33–34
curry, quick, 29–30
and feta stew, 31
in green chili sauce with beans,
35–36
slow cookers, x
stews for, 79–80
sparerib stew, Chinese,
129–30

spinach
beans and, veal and sausage stew
with, 73–74
lentil, and potato stew, 11–12
spring veal ragout, 67–68
spring vegetable(s)
lamb stew with, 103–5
stew, 3–4
stews
freezing, ix, xi
history of, ix
low fat, 123–24
refrigerating, x
Stifado, 79–80
stout, Irish lamb stew with,
109–10
summer vegetable stew, 5
sweet and savory pork stew with
fruit, 119–20

tomato(es)
and corn, monkfish and scallop
stew with, 27–28
sausage and, stew,
121–22
tortillas, 127
Tropp, Barbara, 129

Van Waerebeek, Ruth, 83
veal
    ragout, spring, 67–68
    and sausage stew, with beans and
        spinach, 73–74
    substituting chicken for, 63
veal stew, 59–61
    with carrots, parsnips and
        potatoes, 69–70
    with fennel and mustard,
        65–66
    Marengo, 63–64
    with olives, anchovies, and basil,
        71–72
vegetable stews
    autumn, 7–8
    Greek, 13–14
    spring, 3–4
    summer, 5
    temperature for serving, x
    winter, 9–10
vegetables, blanching, 3
vegetables, spring
    lamb stew with, 103–5
    stew, 3–4
Vegetarian Cooking for Everyone
    (Madison), 3

vegetarians, chili for, 15
Vlaamse Stovery, 83–84

walnuts, 79
Wells, Patricia, 51, 81, 97
wine, xi
    and prunes, chicken with, 49–50
wine, red
    monkfish stewed in, 25–26
    and paprika, pork stew with,
        125–26
    and shiitake mushrooms, beef
        stew with, 85–86
wine, Riesling, chicken with,
    43–44
wine, white, and mustard, beef stew
    with, 81–82
winter vegetable stew, 9–10

yam, pork and, stew with mustard,
    131–32

zucchini, green bean, chickpea, and
    potato stew, 13–14